BAUHAUS

Dedicated to Yael and all my family

NC

BAUHAUS TEL AVIV

AN ARCHITECTURAL GUIDE / NAHOUM COHEN

PHOTOGRAPHS BY JACHIN HIRSCH

BATSFORD

A CIP RECORD FOR THIS BOOK IS AVAILABLE FROM THE BRITISH LIBRARY

PUBLISHED BY B T BATSFORD A member of Chrysalis Books plc
64 BREWERY ROAD, LONDON N7 9NT
WWW.BATSFORD.COM
DESIGN CLAUDIA SCHENK

THIS BOOK HAS BEEN PRODUCED WITH THE KIND ASSISTANCE OF
THE TEL AVIV FOUNDATION

FIRST PUBLISHED 2003

ISBN 0 7134 8792 5

PRINTING AND BINDING IN ITALY

FOR A COPY OF THE BATSFORD CATALOGUE OR INFORMATION
ON SPECIAL QUANTITY ORDERS OF BATSFORD BOOKS PLEASE
CONTACT US ON 020 7697 3000 OR SALES@CHRYSALISBOOKS.CO.UK

Nahoum Cohen 2003

CONTENTS

INTRODUCTION
A LOCAL DEVELOPMENT OF THE MODERN MOVEMENT

Architecture in Israel was and is still influenced by the International Style, and particularly by what is known as the Bauhaus School, modified in various ways to adapt it to local conditions. Walk through Tel Aviv and you will be strolling through the various stages in the development of the International Style. You will also see that the style strongly influences present-day design. It is not too much to claim that the Bauhaus approach provided a necessary injection of vitality during the making of the new country. It began permeating into what was then Palestine under the British Mandate, and developed quickly and strongly in the emerging state of Israel.

FOUNDING OF TEL AVIV

By the end of the 19th century the presence of Zionist ideas was being felt throughout the Jewish world, and especially in Eastern Europe. Jewish people were becoming interested in the old country and in finding ways to better the often desperate conditions in which they lived in Europe. Migration to Palestine was slow at first. There, under Turkish rule, conditions were again very poor, the country being extremely underdeveloped. The empty parts of the coast, near the town of Jaffa, looked very much like a desert, and could be purchased cheaply.

The newcomers had to come through the port of Jaffa, and many stayed there at first. By 1900 there were some 5000 recent immigrants in the new neighbourhoods adjoining Jaffa and to its north. These were largely unplanned, and were neither properly set out nor serviced. Most of the people living there had come from Eastern-European cities. They were well-educated and organised, ready to adopt Zionist ideas, and ready to accept garden-city planning principles, becoming well-known outside Britain by that time.

In 1909 Ahuzat Bait, one of the first new quarters, made up of single-family houses, was given the name of Tel Aviv, which means literally the 'Mount of Spring', and has its origins in the Bible, as well as in the aspirations of Benjamin Z Herzel.

Up to the outbreak of World War I there were no commercial establishments in the new districts. The Turkish authorities were not in favour and tried various means of hindering new building, some, like deportation, undeniably effective. By 1920 some commercial activity had started to the north, and around 2000 new houses were built there. When the British Army conquered Tel Aviv and the Balfour Declaration, allowing for a Jewish homeland in Palestine, was proclaimed, the town was given city status. By 1934 it had grown to 75,000 inhabitants. The expansion was mostly in unplanned neighbourhoods built to a maximum height of two or three storeys.

THE BAUHAUS AND THE INTERNATIONAL STYLE

The Bauhaus School, founded in Weimar in 1919, took as a central tenet that there should be no barrier between the art of design and the ability of the artisan to manufacture. But it did more than that, employing teachers and artists, principally painters with a revolutionary outlook, products of the avant-garde groups that emerged in Europe after World War I. These teachers were developing new aesthetic and philosophical ideas while they were educating aspiring designers. The school survived until the final rise of Nazism in Germany in 1933.

The three directors of the school were architects, all of whom developed new approaches to the built environment. The first, Walter Gropius, believed in space and transparency in architecture. He was not a functionalist, but wanted to see a revolution in the better use of building methods and materials, abandoning useless and cluttering ornament. Hans Mayer, his successor, aspired to the solution of social problems through planning and design. Ludwig Mies van der Rohe, the last head of the school, was not interested in internal architectural solutions or in the balance of space and mass. His aim was to achieve an abstract quality in design, perfection in the execution of details and a very clean look. All these combine in the ideals we identify in the International Style. This comprises simplicity and egalitarianism, rational thought in production, and clarity in the design of buildings and furniture alike. These aims constitute an all-encompassing idealism. The ideas were soon disseminated from central Europe through the USA, Great Britain, South America and, indeed, Palestine. The style is known in Israel as 'Bauhaus' rather than the more correct 'International Style'.

Another influence on young architects came from Le Corbusier: identifiable in the 'pilotis' or exposed columns raising buildings from the ground, in the concrete technology employed, in the use of the roof space, the freedom of the plan and elevations, and the ubiquitous white stucco.

In their seminal book, *The International Style: Architecture Since 1922* (New York 1932), Henry-Russell Hitchcock and Philip Johnson defined three principles or tendencies: 'architecture as volume', rather than as a discipline dealing with the mass of a building; regularity as a virtue in place of symmetry 'or other kinds of obvious balance'; and 'avoidance of applied decoration', depending instead on 'the intrinsic elegance of materials, technical perfection, and fine proportions'. The last was an aspiration only occasionally achieved in Tel Aviv.

ARCHITECTURAL CONTEXT

In the early decades of the twentieth century, design in Palestine tended to be based on traditional Ottoman building styles, with some European eclecticism carried over from the previous century, colonial precedents and neo-romantic influence. In the 1930s attempts to use oriental elements and art-nouveau quotations were made. Designs with Central- and Eastern-European origins were also imported, or even copied.

The styles that were widely employed in the early years of Tel Aviv used a combination of oriental elements such as arches and domes and some Jewish motifs including the seven-branched menora and the Star of David. Eclectic mixtures which borrowed elements from East and West were also popular – the architects Alexander Bervald and Joseph Minor were the chief perpetrators. Other well-known architects of the period were Joseph Berlin, who was influenced by neo-classicism; Tabachnik, influenced by art nouveau; and Yehuda Megidovitz, whose many ideas came from from a mixture of sources. The architecture inflicted on Tel Aviv was far from carrying a new message.

The International Style was introduced into the country by young architects, many of German extraction, some of whom had attended the new Bauhaus school. Most of them came with their families to Palestine, fleeing the rise of Nazism in Germany. In the 1920s and 1930s others came from Russia and Poland, completing their studies in Europe where they absorbed the then emerging ideas of the International Style. They were filled with aspirations, perfectly suited to face the problems and social ideas relating to the creation of a new state for a very old nation, one that had been dispersed around the world for twenty centuries.

The new approach, employing the simple forms of modernity, was swiftly accepted. It fitted the youthfulness – in terms both of age and of outlook – of the people. The will to build a new society uninfluenced by older European traditions readily caught on, and the outstanding new forms of the Bauhaus method were adopted and applied. The main period began around 1935; examples abound in the thousands in Jewish and in some

Arab cities, like Haifa, and in small towns, villages and even *kibutzim*. Our examples are confined to Tel Aviv, which still contains up to one thousand buildings designed in the Bauhaus style.

PLANNING

Tel Aviv grew very quickly, evolving from a small Jaffa neighbourhood of 300 people in 1910 to a town with 150,000 residents by 1945, and with approximately 300,000 by 1999. In 1925 M Dizzengof, then the mayor of Tel Aviv, invited the British planner Patrick Geddes to work on the extensions needed by the new city. Geddes realised that the existing rapidly built neighbourhoods could not easily be altered and concentrated his efforts on establishing a conceptual framework: main roads and public squares providing a matrix for protected residential streets which were to be hard to navigate but quiet and communal, each with a small square or garden, and easily accessed from the commercial thoroughfares.

The influx to the country was so quick and the immigrants had such varied social and cultural backgrounds, as well as economic status, that only a simple plan would be acceptable, and it was adopted by 1929. But the Geddes Plan was adopted as a principle rather than as a set of rules to be applied literally. It was generally implemented although many of its details were abandoned. The small plots and the availability of inexpensive land both helped in the formation of the new city.

By 1938 a new masterplan was needed, raising the density and plot coverage. After preparing a complete study of existing conditions, Geddes proposed a local variation on the garden-city theme with a north-to-south orientation, shading exposed elevations to the south from the sun. The secondary roads with their westerly orientation were to be cooled by breezes from the sea. He established an hierarchy, based on 'main ways' –

where there would be strong vehicular circulation and which would contain most of the city's commercial activity – and on 'home ways', mainly residential, low density, gardened and communal quarters. These streets, arranged in a windmill pattern around a communal space or garden, still perform well. He established a low plot-coverage ratio, around 30 per cent (as opposed to the 60 per cent frequently found in European cities), controlled and manageable small public spaces, and absolutely no row or terrace houses. This last feature contributes greatly to the appearance of Tel Aviv today.

In the Geddes proposal, with its long north-to-south roads, some Arab villages had to be by-passed. The city was poorly connected to the ancient seaport town of Jaffa, which had been generally hostile to the development of Tel Aviv, and to this day the connection is weak. However, judging Geddes' plans with the benefit of hindsight, it does seem that this new and modern city, vibrant and active despite its shortcomings, is one of the few planning successes of the twentieth century.

Geddes' masterplan was a singular attempt to impose the garden-city approach. It proved a suitable environment for Bauhaus-inspired designs using simple geometry to produce inexpensive buildings on small, regular, newly formed parcels of land. The style also proved to be technologically feasible, using plastered and stuccoed block and concrete construction, and not needing the elaborate techniques employed with more traditional, and more expensive, materials.

THE BAUHAUS IN TEL AVIV

Many Tel Aviv architects were students at the Bauhaus school, including Arieh Sharon, Shmuel Mistechkin and Shlomo Berenstein. Others attended the architecture schools in Brussels and Ghent; they included Dov Carmi, Benjamin Aneckstein, Genia Averbuch and

Ben Ami Shulman. Those who went to Italy for their education included Zeev Rechter and Joseph Noifeld.

Recession in the building trade of 1926–29 had encouraged the cleaner (and hence cheaper) approach of the new modernism, which included some art-deco experimentation. Economic depression in Europe accompanied by the triumph of Hitlerism between 1933 and 1937 brought about more changes; some architects left the country because of the difficult times, others left because of the war. This lead to a slowing down in the execution of new designs, few new projects, and very restricted imports of good materials or labour, a situation that persisted almost until 1947.

The society emerging before World War 2 looked for an architectural style suited to its aspirations. Some of the ideas of the Bauhaus suited the new socialist and workers associations (like their counterparts in Europe), who bought and managed big building projects and blocks of communally owned flats. The young architects arriving or returning from Europe wanted to produce a clean architecture with a new look, intended to be humane, egalitarian and democratic. Socialist ideas were rife, and the new ways and methods suited the needs of the working class.

Erich Mendelsohn (1887–1953) introduced a more personal element of expressionism. He opposed the 'emptiness of the simple cube', an approach that derived from cubism in painting but seemed to compromise the freedom of the architect. Mendelsohn first came to Palestine in 1934 and finally left in 1941. In some of the buildings he produced here he introduced curved internal spaces, and this influenced the design perceptions of younger architects. This was generally expressed as a degree of softness in design showing the evidence of a personal touch, with some rounded corners and the use of materials such as stone, instead of the otherwise ubiquitous stucco on concrete.

The square, cubist buildings so often found could be softened and made more varied and detailed. Local architects, led by Richard Kaufman, a friend of Mendelsohn from Berlin, embraced this freedom. They met often to discuss and challenge each other with new ideas. They even had their own magazine, and gained influence in the professional association, as well as in the Town Architect's office.

Joseph Noifeld had also worked with Mendelsohn in Berlin in the 1930s; Mistechkin had been under Mies at the Bauhaus, Berenstein in Le Corbusier's office in Paris with Barkay, Zaki Chelouche and, briefly, Zeev Rechter. Another group was connected to Belgium, included Aneckstein, Averbuch, Shulman, Joseph Cashdan, and Berlin, all working in the modern spirit, and looking for new answers and creative possibilities.

ADAPTING TO LOCAL CONDITIONS

Tel Aviv's weather can be difficult – hot and humid – in summer. This was handled whenever possible by providing lots of shade and natural ventilation, using overhangs, shutters and small window openings sunk into the surface of the wall to reduce glare. Ventilation is possible only when there are westerly winds, and is helped by an open ground floor. Balconies of various sizes and shapes were added.

Materials in the main were based on cement, in the form of different stuccos, plasters and mosaics. Some use was made of steel sections in windows and balustrades. In some respects the materials and techniques used were themselves innovative, especially the mosaics and terrazzo. These were both done in-situ and prefabricated. Sanitary ware was mostly imported, as were mosaic tiles, some of which were very colourful.

The building trade became popular and was adopted by many people, some learning it abroad. Speciality stucco mixtures were imported, sometimes with expert technicians, from Germany, especially the varieties known as the *Waschputz* or *Kratzputz* (washed or brushed external plasters). These are similar to concrete mixtures and they have weathered well. Some metalwork was imported, but more was produced by local craftsmen and iron workers. Steel sections, used in some of the strip windows, were mainly imports. Hard economic times meant that low construction costs were much sought after, as were ways to ameliorate the prevalent humidity and heat.

The new street section was also intriguing for architects, as it permitted higher buildings, raising densities to allow for the influx of newcomers. The main clients for new buildings were small associations of middle-class people, and their use was principally residential. The mixture of different cultures and tastes did not make design decisions easy, nor was it easy to convince people of the benefits one gets from building on stilts. This new way of placing the building had a profound influence on the look of small streets as well as the bigger commercial roads and boulevards, the sites of more expensive structures. One feels that the architects had to work to find a reasonable consensus on these matters, especially on matters of taste.

The roof was very important given the climate and the way of life in the Middle East; it has been so since Biblical days. The use of the roof, shaded in various ways, makes evenings more bearable. Asymmetry was also a debatable feature, and could not be taken for granted. The freedom it granted was important when dealing with small plots, but not all the public was ready to accept it. Designers also had to work with the Bauhaus's 'non-decorative' dictum which meant that functional elements had to serve new aesthetic purposes.

BAUHAUS TEL AVIV NOW

For reasons that remain unclear, though perhaps the uniformity it tended to produce may have been a factor, the Bauhaus style lost its popularity in Israel after the close of World War 2. On the other hand, some of its basic features – the horizontal elements, balconies and flat roofs – continue to have an influence on the architecture of the city to this day.

Tel Aviv itself now has around 400,000 inhabitants, but it is the heart of the densely built-up central part of Israel, almost a 'mega city' of 2.5 million people, and the centre of the cultural and commercial life of the whole country. In the past decade attention has at last been paid to the preservation of individual Bauhaus buildings, and some conception of preserving parts of the urban web is now accepted. In renovating and extending buildings, architects have become very aware of the qualities of the original, and adhere to them. New buildings in Tel Aviv also benefit from the originality of the Bauhaus style – some are even built to look similar to their neighbours, especially in the central core of the city.

That Tel Aviv was built through periods of war and is still suffering from the instability of the region can be seen in the background of poor-quality post-war blocks. And the renovation of Bauhaus buildings tends to be problematic. Some were badly built, with cheap materials. Mistakes in detailing occur frequently. Architects are obliged to invent better detailing, but it has to look like it could have been made 50 years ago. The biggest problems occur because the wrong stuccoes were frequently used. Here, specialist firms, many from Italy, are brought in. Even so poor external-wall construction can prevent proper durable solutions. Also detrimental to the appearance of the city is the effect of piecemeal renovation – but Tel Aviv is by no means the only example of that.

INTRODUCTION

NAMES

Spellings have been chosen to enable names to be read easily. Many street names in Tel Aviv are themselves transliterations from various European languages. 'Square' is used in the same sense as German 'Platz' – an urban space of any shape where people congregate. Documentation of Tel Aviv's architecture in the 1930s is very sparse: it is not always possible to ascribe particular buildings to a particular architect, while some architects are remembered only by their surnames, even their initials having vanished.

PHOTOGRAPHS

As is frequently noted in the text, many of Tel Aviv's Bauhaus buildings are in very poor condition. In these cases, we have retouched the photographs, minimally, to emphasise their enduring qualities rather than their present state.

ACKNOWLEDGEMENTS

Most of the photographs in this book are by Jachin Hirsch; most of the pictures of details are by the author. Black-and-white archive photographs are by Isaac Kalter, from the Kalter Collection. The photographs of 1 Frug Street are from Arieh Sharon's book, *Kibbutz and Bauhaus*. The plans and elevations have been drawn by Felix Scheinkerman.

The person responsible for the interest and revival in the efforts to conserve both particular buildings and Bauhaus design at the urban scale is the architect Nitza Szmuk. Her excellent book, *Batim min Haholl* (*Built of Sand*), is a complete compilation of the Bauhaus experience in Tel Aviv. The present author owes much to this volume.

The Tel Aviv Foundation and in particular its director, David Hernich, were enthusiastically helpful from the start of my work on this book.

5 FRUG STREET

YEHUDA LIOLKA 1936

HOUSING

10 AARONOVITZ STREET

A residential building with three or four flats on each floor in a north-central part of Tel Aviv developed in the mid 1930s. Both the size and form of the building are impressive. The entrance is not prominent and the garden is dominated by the ground floor and by the volumes developed above it. The main mass comprises overpoweringly sculptural geometric cylinders, rendered even more effective by the balconies and the recesses they form, producing the contrasts of light and shadow that are characteristic of the style. The decorative line is developed by the horizontal balustrades. Most openings are recessed into the balconies, which provide welcome shade.

Proportions are well handled through the whole volume, not just on the elevations. This is a good example of extended geometry, reaching out of the normal flat, square box.

Like much of Tel Aviv's Bauhaus heritage, this building has not been renovated for the last 30 years and as a result does not look its best. It illustrates the state of many similar buildings.

(Plan, see page 239.)

Hausman & Barzilai 1937

49 AHAD HA'AM STREET

This was one of the first successful attempts at the complete renovation of a Bauhaus-style building in Tel Aviv, following an earlier period in which new technological solutions to the problems of ageing fabric – some were built using very cheap and poor-quality concrete blocks – had been tried out. Care has been taken to remain faithful to the original building, down to its colours and the textures of finishes. New windows correspond to the old ones; the correct external plaster has been used.

The building is a common type, a typical Tel Aviv condominium with around ten flats. It was built close to Rothschild Boulevard on a corner plot of about 400 square metres, in a neighbourhood that was fashionable from the founding of Tel Aviv through the period of its early expansion. The main bulk of the building hints at a corner composition with rounded volumes attempting to smooth the angle. Some of the shapes are slightly odd, especially the cut cylinder at the back. The garden is small and not especially interesting, and not enough attention has been paid to the front garden wall and a small net fence nearby.

The external finish is the normal coloured flat local stucco, with large fenestration and a few blinds. The windows have some horizontal protection against glare. Balconies are disproportionate and their horizontal balustrades are neither decorative nor even stylistically integrated with the main bulk. Internally, some rooms are oddly shaped because of the rounded external walls. The general proportions are a little squat and not well developed vertically. The flat roof is not very useful and perhaps not even useable.

This small building has an original shape, developed along period lines, with some curious innovations in the unusually worked out geometric horizontal features. It remains unfortunate that the shape does not fully engage organically with its corner plot, and does not relate at all to nearby buildings.

(Plan, see page 240.)

Zaki Chelouche 1933

57 AHAD HA'AM STREET

Genia Averbuch (1909–77) was born in Russia and came to Palestine at the age of three. She studied in Rome, Brussels and Ghent. By 1934 she had won first prize in the competition for the design of Dizengof Square. After 1945 she dealt mainly with public buildings, paying a lot of attention to detailing and quality of execution. One of the most prominent women architects of her time, she also had a wide variety of private clients and was a pioneer in developing the new role of the architect.

Ahad Ha'am Street, parallel to Rothschild Boulevard, was popular with Bauhaus designers. A one-way street, it leads from Allenby Street to the Habima National Theatre in the north. Its narrowness makes it difficult to appreciate the good buildings along it. Little refurbished in the past twenty years, Averbruch's building at No. 57 has one balcony in the front crudely closed up, spoiling the original proportions. A single-family house, it contains three spacious apartments.

The mass of the building is presented as a powerful cubist aesthetic exercise. While not unusual for its time, it is a little too influenced by theory to be entirely successful as livable architecture. It still has a good presence, appearing 'clean and well handled'. The slightly expressionist cubes are well proportioned and the front stairs have a simplicity that benefits the composition. No garden was planned, and the wall and basement constitute the base of the composition. The forceful box-shaped negative volume of the entry plays an essential role in rendering the volumes plastic, as does the vertical window of the stairway. The proportions of the openings are dictated by formal considerations, and are very graphically, even flatly handled. Balustrades offer minimal decorative relief.

The simplicity of handling makes this a unique example of the style. It is certainly unfortunate that the shape should be spoiled by the closed-up first-floor balcony, but it is very hard to enforce conservation within current building law.

Genia Averbuch 1934

93 AHAD HA'AM STREET

Zeev Rechter (1898–1960) started his professional education in Russia and completed it in Rome where he had the first inklings of the rising modernism. He came to Palestine in 1919. By 1929 he was studying again, this time in Paris where he was enthused by the teachings of Le Corbusier. He was one of the founders of the local Association of Architects. His work shows cubist influence, and he was one of the first architects to place a house on piloti. He raised a son and a grandson as architects, and they continue his work.

A three-storey residential condominium, 93 Ahad Ha'am Street is sited in a popular neighbourhood with many similarly sized houses. It has a simple cube shape, unspoiled by additional volumes and without any of the 'sculptural' effects that were sometimes employed. The entrance is not stressed, nor indeed are the garden or the boundary. Part of the ground floor is used commercially.

Designed as an inexpensive-looking working-class block, its four-room flats are far from typical and were originally hardly affordable. The main elevations are relieved a little by the balconies and balustrades, the materials being stucco and painted steel.

Interiors are minimal and not very high. Openings are small but adequate, perhaps appropriate for the economic class for which the building was designed. The proportions of the big balconies speak for themselves. They are the only lavish element of the design, and aesthetically formed in the Bauhaus style, that is in simple, shaded volumes, shaped by the geometric slab projections and planes. It is worth noting precisely because of these forms, which are very characteristic of the period.

Cleaning up the façades and minor refurbishment of the exterior has been enough to restore the beauty and originality of the building.

(Plan, see page 241.)

Zeev Rechter 1937

95 AHAD HA'AM STREET

Shlomo Berenstein (1907–69) was born in Vilnius and came to Palestine in 1924 to complete his studies at the Haifa Technion. He also studied at the Bauhaus school, where he was cited as a good pupil of Mies van der Rohe, and worked in Le Corbusier's office in Paris. His speciality was private housing, but he also had a period as an architect employed by the municipal authority of Tel Aviv.

His building at 95 Ahad Ha'am Street was successfully renovated during the 1990s, initiating a movement in the neighbourhood that culminated in the renewal, with some modestly scaled new construction, of a dense midtown area that had been neglected since the 1950s.

This is a residential building with commercial use on the ground floor and good access offered by a corner site. It contains six or seven apartments and a useable roof. Surrounded by similar-sized blocks on small (350-square-metre) plots, it owes its originality to a simple and effective design. Formally speaking, we have here a rectangular and cubic shape, with two of its elevations fully exposed to the main and side streets. The streets, which are orthogonal and narrow (10 to 12 metres wide), do not allow much of a view. A tiny garden faces the entrance. This is a formal composition using openings and flat stucco surfaces treated according to their proportions.

Some relief is attempted in the prefabricated balustrades, an unusual achievement among these early experiments in concrete building technology, and one that proved an important precedent in detailing locally. The fenestration of the stairwell is used in the composition, and helps to give some depth to the otherwise flat surfaces. Depth is also achieved by the structure on the roof, treated as a roof garden providing shade (it is not actually used). The flat proportions have some drama and are arranged off-centre, thus introducing a degree of personal expression. The balconies are recessed and can be con-

Shlomo Berenstein 1937

sidered as rooms without the protection of windows – an optimistic move in the design of these elements, especially as far as the weather is concerned. Subsequently, most of these balcony rooms have been enclosed – the original intention of the architect can be clearly seen in the archive photograph opposite. This has happened to many other similar buildings, as the number of habitable rooms was never adequate.

מעדנים צ. רוטשטין תוצרת חלב

126 AHAD HA'AM STREET

126 Ahad Ha'am Street has been well maintained through the years. Nevertheless it has recently been renovated when another floor was successfully and inconspicuously added. A corner residential block with unusually big three- and four-room apartments, it has had wealthier occupants than many other buildings, a fact which has helped its upkeep. It contains nine or ten apartments, with a penthouse contributing to the quality of maintenance at roof level.

On its corner site, its bulk slightly raised from the level of the street and recessed at the entrance, the building achieves a suitably dramatic effect. An imposing and somewhat austere shape, it is open to the north-west to allow the wind to penetrate. The entrance is further accentuated by the position and separation of the garden's retaining wall, which delimits a protected area which benefits the trees here. The raised ground floor is rather like a first floor in its relationship to the street. The special stucco, containing a medium-size pebble and slightly dashed, is an off-white/soft yellow colour and has maintained its appearance for many years.

Interiors are unusually spacious, relatively speaking. Openings and proportions are 'strip' oriented into the bulk of the two main cubes, which are offset from one another. No other decoration has been permitted – hence the austere character of the composition. The lack of balustrades and balconies seen in the building today supports the intentions of the architect, despite the fact that the original deeply recessed balcony areas were only later enclosed as rooms.

(Plan, see page 242.)

Dov Carmi 1935

24 BALFOUR STREET

A big block, very substantial for its period, containing about 16 spacious and well-designed flats for middle-class residents.This is an exceptional building for the austere period in which it was built, and it has been reasonably well looked after. The plot size is bigger than normal, around 650 square metres. It is situated on a street connecting the residential Rothschild Boulevard to the principal commercial thoroughfare, Allenby Street. With an imposing façade on Balfour Street, it looks rather like a building for public use. Entrance is through a well-proportioned garden running the whole length of the front of the site. Most of the ground floor is devoted to the entrance hall, which has interior-design elements typical of the Bauhaus approach, such as the fenestration – which is nicely detailed in wood and has some specially formed decorative glass – coloured tiles and stair balustrades.

Externally, the scraped stucco is in good condition, having been well executed with sound plaster mixes. The roof has a cast-concrete pergola to provide shade. These roofs proved to be not entirely successful: communal life did not develop on the rooftops as the architects had intended. Residents declined to climb up there to sit in the cool during the summer, preferring to stay in their flats.

Balconies have square proportions, and the volumetric composition is only relieved by the roof element and two entrance halls.

The whole reads like a well-proportioned horizontally oriented volume, with an air of decent living, a feature prominent in the Bauhaus residential designs of the period. This feeling is greatly helped by the decorative open balconies, which are often the sole relief to the inherent austerity of the style.

(Plan, see page 243.)

Shmuel Plato 1935

3 BEN AMI STREET

Few Bauhaus buildings are completely symmetrical. One of the sculptural premises of the movement was that forms were seen in the round and therefore could never be appreciated from an axial or frontal point of view. Furthermore, the modern forms of design were, to a degree, expressionist. Self-expression was regarded as dynamic, new, futuristic, and therefore demanding suitably asymmetrical multi-faceted forms.

However, there are certain conditions that permit or encourage symmetry. A double block on a wide plot of land with a central approach is intrinsically suitable for such a treatment. Symmetry could also stem from the influence of Middle-Eastern dwellings, with a central hall and living space flanked on both sides with bedrooms. Examples of such dwellings exist in great numbers in Beirut, Damascus and Jerusalem, among many other cities.

The recently renovated house at 3 Ben Ami Street is a good example of this. The symmetrical form is topped by a clean rectangle on the roof and enlivened by the rounded volume there. The well-placed balconies and balustrades, the middle one with an atypical oval shape, create an effective focal point. The garden and the palm trees add charm to the composition. This is an event in the street, well seen from both sides, and a relatively opulent example of the Bauhaus in Tel Aviv.

Mordechai Rosengarten 1936

13 BEN GURION BOULEVARD

Not many town houses were designed in the International Style in Tel Aviv, but this is one of the few. Built as late as 1954, it is quite purist in its elements. It has been well kept, a must in the harsh climate near the sea, and as a result it looks almost fresh. A private residence for a well-off family, it has around 600 square metres of floor space. The building faces the boulevard which ends close by to the west, at the seafront. The neighbourhood, well to the north of town, was not developed until the 1950s, and has the typical mix: a main commercial street bordering small residential districts made up entirely of parcels of 350 square metres, covered in regular blocks of flats, three to four storeys high. This composition does not look out of place, and takes a simple block as its theme.

The main street façade shows a bulky rectangular box, relieved on the top by an open colonnaded balcony and roof terrace. Two large openings, placed diagonally and symmetrically on the elevation, show a dramatic sense of proportion. The principle of unadorned design employed here is really a modernist one, an outcome of basic Bauhaus principles that have remained productive.

The front garden is simply handled so as not to encumber the design; the side entrance is similarly muted. Surfaces are a simple brushed stucco, applied well, which has a lively texture in the strong local sunlight.

One may feel that there is an air of officialdom about the building, even an inappropriate functionality. What may be lacking is a touch of freedom, some sign of life in the perfection of the building's geometry.

Dov Carmi 1954

212–214 BEN YEHUDA STREET

A fine example of a twin residential building on a commercial main street in the north of Tel Aviv. There are six apartments on each side. The buildings are elevated from street level by the wide central open stairway. This achieves a somewhat monumental effect, enhanced by the pronounced symmetry of the two blocks which mirror each other.

There is good separation from the busy road. The central space created by the division of the two main cubes makes for a strong presence on the street and adds to the public area. The garden is on a higher level, contained by the retaining wall which faces the sidewalk. It partially hides the balconies of the ground-floor flats, the only balconies, but they are unusually spacious and well protected. The dwellings are bigger than was normal at the time of construction because the building is on an atypically large plot.

The composition is also unusual as it has some cubist characteristics but with the rare addition of symmetry. The design uses a smaller cube projecting out of a basic, bigger parental one. The effect is enhanced by the strip windows along the full width of the elevation and an overhang above the ground-floor balconies. This formation makes for some striking proportions which compensate for the neglected exterior and upkeep. The roof is not included in the design and is not used. A single *Washingtonia* palm tree towers over the ensemble, and is a reminder of the fact that we are in a hot Mediterranean region.

The presence of a large plot with a wide street front is an indication that an alternative way to plan Tel Aviv, with bigger parcels of land, could have produced a better-looking environment, especially in residential districts. However, the capital needed for such an approach was not readily available.

The archive photographs show similar but less-successful examples of symmetry.

Benjamin Aneckstein and Z Baron 1935

2 AHAD HA'AM STREET

SCHMUEL STEINBOK 1936

29 GORDON STREET

LOUIS REDSTONE 1936

18 BIALIK STREET

Bialik Street leads to a number of important public buildings and museums, most dating to the 1920s and '30s. The stylistic mixture reveals the influences brought from Central Europe and their modern interpretation, with the addition of some local colour.

No. 18 is an exceptionally well-built house for its period, standing on a double-sized plot. The building has been well taken care of, and some major repairs have been carried out. It has been always in residential use, though some general practitioners have had their private clinics here alongside their homes, a common arrangement for doctors here. Separate entrances to the practices were included in the original plans. There are nine apartments, most of them quite spacious, with up to six rooms. The connection to the clinic is usually through a dining area.

The composition is formed by the two masses of the wings. These are connected and split, creating a garden in a dynamic space enclosed by the rounded volumes. The garden enhances both entrances, with the space on the plot providing an unusual opening in the street frontage. The ground-floor flats have no access to the common garden.

The volumes created are extraordinary. The one on the left is animated by the round solid with the bands of curved balconies and their precise geometry. The other has only corner balconies with rounded balustrades. The effect is unique in spite of the familiarity of all the details, windows and materials. The stucco used is of very good quality and workmanship, hard to find locally. It is of washed small-aggregate concrete, the stone being multi-coloured. The round front rooms are unusual both in their proportions and in the wooden window frames and jalousie blinds.

Proportions are rather low and only slightly relieved by the lighted stairwell. This is a common feature in Bauhaus buildings, where the emphasis on horizontality can produce a squat effect.

Friedman Bros 1935

17 EMILE ZOLA STREET

A corner residential building made up of eight three-roomed flats, with roof access from those at the top. This is a successful renovation done in 1995 with full respect for the original design. The building was always intended for residential use and the number of apartments has not been altered, maintaining a density characteristic of this relatively well-to-do middle-class district. Its current inhabitants – most of them in their thirties when they settled here in the 1950s and with similar backgrounds and education – had small families, typically two or three children. The district borders on two commercial thoroughfares, Dizengof Street to the east and Ben Yehuda Street to the west. The block sizes are relatively modest, around 60 by 40 metres, resulting in an intimate scale which is immediately apparent.

The mass of the building has its slim flank elevation facing Ben Gurion Boulevard, while the main elevation is on the side street. This is narrow, a result of the Geddes Plan in which local residential and internal streets are kept small to discourage traffic, creating a quiet ambience in a busy central part of town.

A simple stucco rectangular block, well finished and carrying a few simple recessed lines in the plaster, it looks elegant. Steel balustrades add some colour and relief. The ground floor is used for dwellings, while the garden offers some protection. The composition is carried through by the typically rounded shape of the corner balconies. The stepped section of the balcony carries a recess for flowerpots, a feature that was often attempted but usually failed because of bad detailing. The successful ones tend to be over-colourful. The openings are carefully placed and balanced in their execution and finish. The roof, part of which is used as a garden, contributes to the relaxed appearance of this building.

H Sima and A Glik 1935

5 ENGEL STREET

A very typical small-scale interpretation of the International Style, exhibiting most of the available elements and quite effective in the strongly contrasting light and shade of seaside Tel Aviv. Standing in a quiet but central neighbourhood, the building uses its main balconies to get the sea breeze, very important in the hot and humid summers here, and which explains the similar orientation of all the openings in the recessed volumes.

Architect Sam Barkay was employed in Le Corbusier's office in Paris before he came to Tel Aviv. The small unprotected balcony, unusual in its formal conception, may be a small reminder of this. In its dramatic simplicity, the rest of the building is also reminiscent of some of Le Corbusier's sketches. The roof's concrete pergola (a difficult structure to maintain) is also dramatic and contributes strongly to the whole. The roof does not seem to have been communally or even privately used – the weather is too harsh in summer, despite the minimal shade. Stronger protection is needed but rarely provided.The glass wall of the stairway is another familiar element, furnishing lots of light to the stairs.

The precise forms of the Bauhaus need a strong and resistant stucco, difficult to obtain and hard to execute. In the strong perpendicular sunlight, every small fault in the vertical planes of the walls is exaggerated tenfold. It is almost impossible to create a flat non-textured surface under such conditions, and the years have done much damage. Furthermore, open balconies adjoining the small flats have been closed to add to the useable floor space. Various unsuitable methods and materials have been employed, all detrimental to the almost obsessively clean design.

Sam Barkay 1934

1 FRANKFURT STREET

Situated on a residential side street in northern Tel Aviv, this building had been neglected since the 1950s but was given a new lease of life in 1999. The renovation has been entirely successful, in that it does not show any trace of the new techniques and materials used. This is not an easy task, especially as European restoration know-how is lacking locally. As the entire building was in a very poor state, the interiors were completely redesigned, but without harming the front elevations.

The revival in the care of old buildings and all it means over the last decade stems partly from increased awareness, new bye-laws, some return of population to the city, and the dedication of architects in the planning department. Sometimes these factors can produce results like this modest but striking example of the International Style. The effect is achieved mainly through the materials used, and the readiness to spend the money necessary. Here, washed and granulated stucco on the main body of the building and a plain off-white plaster (reinforced with glass and resins and prefabricated in the renovation) on balustrades and balconies both perform well.

Horizontal lines are dominant in this building, as usual, and they are balanced by the stairwell window, accentuating the cube by turning sideways on to the roof. This was a popular operation for Bauhaus-influenced architects. A row of small round openings – another element often found in Bauhaus buildings with origins in industrial design and nautical shapes – adds a touch of decoration to the composition.

The residential nature of this corner building is emphasised by its balconies: there is no mistaking the function we are facing.

Zvi Spokoini 1937

49 FRISHMAN STREET

Mixed residential and commercial use on a corner where two noisy streets meet. The building was refurbished externally in the last decade.

Judged on the local scale, this is an imposing building, helped by the fact that it forms a recessed street corner. The simple, pleasingly proportioned cube is successful because of the carefully balanced sizes of openings. The new aesthetic represented by this building still conveys the appearance of efficiency, but a lot, as usual, depends not only on the style chosen but on the personality and talent of the architect.

The ground-floor shops, normally considered a problem in buildings like this, have a minimal presence. The roof contributes to the composition, not by its use, but because a concrete beam surrounding the contour hints at a possible extension or roof garden. This sort of motif was often used as an expressive form, giving shape to a striking composition, not always with function in mind, but purely as a formal design element.

The deep recess of the balconies is almost abstract as well. They are very effective as areas of shade in the clean form, and give some transparency to the block.

The building touches the sidewalk brusquely and bluntly, not hiding behind the niceties of a garden or private useable space. It is seen as a clear and precise shape which helps the clarity of the road junction, an entirely urban spatial creation.

Benjamin Aneckstein 1936

רח' ריינס
REINES
20
אריאל

1 FRUG STREET

Arieh Sharon (1900–80) was born in Poland and came to Tel Aviv in 1920, to a kibbutz. By 1926 he was at the Bauhaus school in Dessau. Educated by teachers like Klee, Albers, and Kandinsky, he graduated in 1929. He was in private practice soon after, where he designed some important public and residential buildings. He had some teaching experience in the Technion, alongside a fruitful career and prolific public work.

Many of his town-planning ideas were published and internationally known, and his belief in Bauhaus principles provided the ideological background to his practice, which was instrumental in introducing those ideas into the process of forming the new country. His thinking, buildings and design attitudes were avant-garde for the time, and his success may be regarded as proving the value of his beliefs. One of his major achievements was the introduction, in those early years of Tel Aviv, of flats for the working class, and here he was assisted by various labour union organisations. These blocks contain small two-room flats, simply designed and well-built, which proved adequate for families without much capital in a struggling emigrant country. The proportions are based on a European four-sided closed block with a communal garden in the middle, offering good ventilation and some sun protection in the sub-tropical climate. They are normally three-storey, on an open ground-floor plan which provides beneficial shade and cooling breezes. Interiors are very basic, even austere in their organisation and potential, and necessarily economical in area. The upkeep of the garden was done by communal effort and enjoyed by all.

The success of these projects owed something to their relatively good position in the north part of Tel Aviv, far from poor and problematic districts like Jaffa. The inhabitants were well aware of the new socialist direction of their lives and prospects; most of them were educated and brought up in Zionist-organised youth movements with a working-

Arieh Sharon 1936

class outlook, leftist and modern. This is in marked contrast to their badly formed counterparts in poorer districts, where workers were not well organised, nor educated in this way, with the new energies necessary for an old nation. In more impoverished districts in the south of Tel Aviv, badly designed neighbourhoods were formed at the same time. Often owned by absentee landlords, they were a product of nineteenth-century practices, and they remain contentious to this day. Tel Aviv is a showcase of the way town planning is a expression of beliefs and social practices.

The internally oriented communal space, new even for similar buildings in Europe, was a fresh experiment in architectural terms, made with care and hope. The flats – two to each floor – are not very well-ventilated, with only a slight attempt at providing through-ventilation although this can be essential in the Tel Aviv area, which can be stifling.

The simple composition is helped by balconies, strip windows, and shaded and inviting colonnades. The small flats, necessarily cheap when they were built, proved to be problematic 50 years later when standards of living rose significantly. Furthermore, the flats were a uniform size. By the 1980s they were rented out, not normally considered to be a socialist practice, but one which quickly led to misuse and deterioration, something that could have been anticipated. The inevitable happened: strangers moved in; the balconies closed; the communal garden was neglected. Today the project is almost unrecognisable.

18 GEORGE ELIOT STREET

A good example of one of the central themes of the new architecture of the 1930s – the use of steel technology in combination with glass. As machines could turn out useful steel profiles for fenestration, factories began to provide prefabricated parts that excited the imagination of young architects and were widely employed to create new imagery.

One example was the fenestration of vertical staircases, which soon took on the appearance of, and were called, thermometers, denoting verticality and subdivision. At the time, this was a high-tech application and it acquired almost symbolic status. To achieve machine-made precision of a design element, a repeatable, industrially manufactured part whose quality could be pre-ordered and even priced, was previously unheard of by the architectural avant-garde. The fact that these elements could be backlit at night, and thus offered a new way of having a prominent light source calling attention to a building, was a further attraction. These light signs soon became the symbols of new design.

In the case of this building, a conspicuous residential block, the thermometer is placed right at the corner.

A Berger and I Mandelbaum 1935

12 GOTTLIEB STREET

Haim Cashdan (1906–58) was born in Jaffa and educated in Brussels. He worked in various countries in the Middle East and by 1937 was in private practice with his brother, Joseph. Among his achievements was the introduction and practice of modern building methods in his work for the government. Joseph Cashdan (1910–55) was educated at the Haifa Technion and joined his brother in many residential projects. He left Israel in the 1940s for the United States.

12 Gottlieb Street is an outstanding composition by the brothers. The art-deco influence which is discernible can be ascribed to Haim's time in Brussels. It is an ordinary small block of flats in a quiet one-way street in north-central Tel Aviv. The main elevation is difficult to see well, in fact it is not immediately apparent, and its effect is a little lost on the passer-by. But it is a completely off-centre asymmetrical composition, a somewhat eccentric building because of the elements and styles not normally seen together.

The round windows of the stairwell, whose source is undoubtedly marine (an influence widely used in the machine age), are very like portholes, with orthogonal strips running alongside the well. Two very singular types of balconies have been combined: one with an horizontal overhang, the other semicircular in plan. While both elements are very much elements of the style, they are seldom used together. The balconies include specially formed boxes to contain flowerpots (but they do not stand up well to the water collecting in them) and they are decorated with horizontal steel strips. The round-shaped balconies on the left are topped by a genuine art-deco three-pronged vertical strip to the roof. This completely decorative element is very much like 'brooch' ornament, and it has had an occasional postmodern revival.

Haim and Joseph Cashdan 1937

79 GORDON STREET

An building illustrating early steps in the invention and use of the elements that characterise the Bauhaus style. Although it is not in the best repair, it is worth pointing out as an excellent compilation of details.

Gordon Street leads from the beach to Rabin Square, Tel Aviv's principal square, in front of the town hall. A common small block of flats stands on a raised base at the south-eastern corner. The side street leads into a small public garden.

The elevations have innovative details. The stairwell window has proportions which do not correspond to the volumes or other elements in the building. The roof is reached through the concrete pergola, an element that helps to unify the design. The balconies have simple and effective balustrades, horizontal steel bars producing an effect of transparency. The smaller balconies are unique and striking. The garden balustrade, running horizontally along the garden wall as well, is a part of the whole. While windows, balconies, and balustrades are not integrated in terms of size, the proportions of the façades make the whole composition work. It is the play of surfaces rather than of volumes that is evident here. The architect successfully pulls of a feat, often attempted, on a site too small for the deployment of a large or three-dimensional composition.

(Plan, see page 244.)

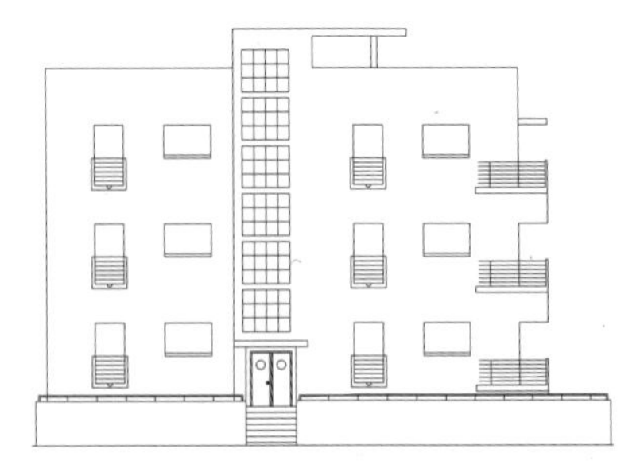

Sam Barkay 1935

54 HAMELEH GEORGE STREET

A culmination of the attempt to soften the hard edges of the machine-age aspects of the International Style.

The whole front part of the building facing the big and noisy Hameleh (King) George Street is turned into a wavy strip of balconies (enclosed at a later stage), an element which is easier to elaborate upon than an orthogonal geometry. The five 'waves' are of the same size, the corner ones turning into Dizengof Street. The fact that the ground floor is for commercial use helps in lending some lightness to the otherwise massive bulk of the building. The flat shop windows serve as a contrasting backdrop to the solid wave of the floors above.

The building has been renovated, and it shows. Located on an important corner, it plays an important role in Tel Aviv's urban look.

Zeev Haller 1936

לשירותך תמיד

52 HASHMONAIM STREET

The physical presence of this residential block is greatly enhanced by the cantilevered balconies, sustained right on a corner with Rothschild Boulevard. The composition is very simple and the number of elements or variations used has been kept to a minimum. The restrained garden and a good entrance under the canopy of the balcony support the impression of simplicity.

It shows the effectiveness of design influenced chiefly by freedom and ability exercised on the projecting elements, where the engineering is largely unhindered by the demands of function. These daring forms play an essential role in achieving a sense of well-being for residents.

Schmuel Steinbok 1935

18 HESS STREET

Amazingly, this simple, clean and unpretentious residential building has withstood the vagaries of time. It has no additions, no changes, no closed balconies, no air-conditioning units, and it looks almost as fresh as when it was newly built.

The vertical slit separating the two blocks uses the stairway for the purposes of formal composition. The wall facing the street near the recessed entrance is the most typically modelled with the cut-out appearance characteristic of the style.

The careful proportions of the windows and the lines of the balconies are exemplary. Because of the complete lack of ornament, the basic principles of the design are clearly read. However, the barrenness of the forms and the unmitigated exposure to glare are too brutal.

Genia Averbuch before 1938

18

2 HISSIN STREET

Topographical conditions have dictated that some buildings are erected on a podium, with a retaining wall facing the street. This is not always very welcome, as the wall becomes a blind border to the sidewalk, and this is especially noticeable in a city without many hilly sites. At the corner with Hissin Street, Dizengof Street becomes the steepest road in town and offers this side view of a building which seems taller than it really is.

The building, which cries out for renovation, was built as flats for families coming from different backgrounds but all faced with a common fate; not an easy programme in a country continually changing and challenged by social conditions. The attitude of inhabitants to their flats is a mixture of the attitudes of peoples with very different assumptions. Most of them were and are not interested in the external appearance of a jointly owned building. That would mean reaching a consensus and understanding one's neighbours, and that has not yet happened. The result is a product of various levels of misuse and faulty upkeep, with the external spaces treated as various residents have seen fit. It is only inside the private habitat of the flat that one finds more civility.

Exposure to the busy and noisy street has not benefitted the building.

In terms of design, it is a square block in which the stairwell is used as an accent, turning on the roof to form a protected exit. Technically, the balustrades on the balconies and roof represent an advanced solution. Their horizontal slits indicate an attempt to facilitate ventilation.

The garden is not much used at present, and the feeling is one of over-use of the plot (which is just 400 square metres). The protection offered by overhangs – present only on the upper floor – is insufficient. It is clear that users have gone to extreme lengths to shelter themselves from sun and rain.

Zvi Spokoini 1934

65 HOVEVEI ZION STREET

The happy position of this building adds to its own excellence and outstanding presence. It stands on the corner of a double-sized plot and it fronts an intimate public square and small garden. Three sides of the building are offered to view – the architecture performs its role in the formation of protected and well-articulated public space. The onlooker feels that he is taken into account by the design, accepted and offered a meeting space, a basic forum. This is achieved before the articulation of the building begins to happen. As an attitude, however, it helps the designer to put his case clearly, the stage being fully set, illuminated and made negotiable to the public.

The strong contrast of light and shade helps to build a dramatic, clean Bauhaus shape, especially as the finishes and the building's greenish colour have withstood the wear of the last 60 years (the green, not a common Bauhaus colour, has Eastern connotations). The small front garden does not hamper the view, as often happens in similar situations.

The size of the plot allows for three generously sized flats on each of three floors, apart from a well-used and lit cellar and a roof flat. One wing has four-roomed apartments; another wing with a separate entry and staircase has smaller, three-roomed flats. Rooms are spacious (at least 4 by 4 metres), well-ventilated and lit. Most flats of this period were small (an average of just 50 square metres) and often had only two bedrooms, so these flats are not typical. Tel Aviv is still suffering from the inadequate size of its flats, which makes regeneration of the urban centre difficult.

The building surrounds an external fire-escape stairway, formed into the court space, through which the kitchens and service rooms are ventilated. This is not the happiest solution because the result is to constrain the internal layout and position of these rooms. The living room connects to the master bedroom which has double doors and

Pinhas Hutt 1935

41-639-15

offers the possibility of having a larger dayroom. This was often done using double, sliding and room-dividing doors.

The external composition is striking. The main balcony is rounded with a different external balustrade, forming a spacious corner. The other two wings, ending in balconies, act as effective backdrops. They are less open, but their projecting corners turn well.

The external finish is a coloured concrete terrazzo-type mixture, incorporating coloured pebbles, exposed and brushed. It is very well preserved, proving the importance of using a finish that is suitable for the climate. Although expensive, it has paid for itself.

Pinhas Hutt 1935

14 IDELSON STREET

Designed by one of the outstanding young architects to emigrate to Palestine, this is another building that has not been well maintained but its detailing is worth looking into. The simple block has a recessed secondary wing with a round balcony allowing another flat to be sited on the same floor but still facing the front. This is a strategy often employed locally as the flat at the back of the block was always considered more difficult to sell. A balcony or at least a window on the front street elevation offers better ventilation and a good prospect for a potential purchaser.

The effectiveness of the composition is enhanced, as so often, by the slight recessed slit of the stairwell.

The balustrades of the front balconies are unusual horizontal concrete rails encasing steel mesh and a small beam. Carefully made, they have withstood exposure to the weather over more than 60 years. The two balconies and balustrades differ slightly, a subtlety in the design approach that makes it successful.

The street is close to one of the busiest places in Tel Aviv – commercial Ben Yehuda Street near the important Mougrabi Square.

Zeev Haller 1936

תחנת
מוניות
מוניות
TAXI

25 IDELSON STREET

With its strategic position on a hill, this building acts as a local landmark. It stands at the junction of three streets, the entrance being from the quiet side street. The building has been well maintained as it has not been divided into flats although for a time it was used as offices (a fate which overtook many local residential buildings). Fortunately this did not do much harm. It is protected from its neighbours by the topography and tall walls. The unusually large site (866 square metres) helps as well, and allows for a bigger composition without interference from party walls. It has been designed as a statement of modernity with subtle Middle-Eastern overtones, especially the impressive overhangs that protect the strip windows from midday glare.

A three-dimensional and free development of the Bauhaus theme gives this urban villa a graceful form, helped by the generous garden. Internal divisions hint at a range of various-sized dwellings with ample proportions, but it was used mainly as a family home. Some balconies are recessed and pragmatically protected. The ground floors have access to the back gardens while the main entrance is formal, placed at the junction of the two cubes that form the wings. The garden has its original front car gate, not a typical feature in this type of dwelling.

The addition of external air-conditioning units is a serious and recurring blight, not only in Tel Aviv of course. Many attempts have been made to find a suitable hiding place or a less intrusive design for them.

The flat stucco plaster looks well applied. The main surfaces are broken up by projections, which makes the stucco easier to apply and maintain.

(Plan, see page 245.)

Richard Kaufman 1931

29 IDELSON STREET

Dov Carmi (1905–62), was born in Odessa and had emigrated to Palestine by 1921. He studied painting at the Bezalel School in Jerusalem and had completed his architectural education in Ghent by 1930. In a brief but brilliant career, Carmi designed more than 200 buildings. He is known for his search for perfection in the elevations, proportions and detailing of his buildings. He succeeded in finding the elusive way to turn the practical and functional into the beautiful, managing to temper the austerity of modernism by unobtrusive and decorative handling of details. He was followed and admired by many of the younger generation, and today his son and daughter are both well-known architects in Tel Aviv.

The details of the entry pergola are a good way into the design of this building. It leads into a colourful light stairwell, equipped with a well-finished balustrade.

The west elevation shows a mildly expressionist departure from the usual right angles of the formal Bauhaus approach. The main elevation, with the recessed bigger volume, shows strip windows and balconies at their best, while the west elevation is treated diagonally, helping the combination to reach into the back volume.

The forms are not bold, but their elaboration is powerful because of the sureness of the building's proportions. The whole is a bold statement of three-dimensionality.

Dov Carmi 1936

3 MAPU STREET

The way monumentality is introduced into this simple block of flats is illuminating, in that it shows that monumentality is not only a matter of size. The feat is achieved by a series of extreme decisions. Firstly, the walls are treated as separate planes and surfaces. They do not support anything at all. They look like the sides of a box, weightless; in principle they could be opened or dismantled at will. Secondly, the strip windows cut into the walls are also extensions of the balustrades. Furthermore, the wall extends down to act like a brise-soleil. Then the volume is cut and broken in two, one part raised half a storey.

The composition is cubist and precise. Moves are apparent and studied. Some of the walls near the entrance break just hang in space as vertical projecting surfaces. The balustrades and roof beams limit the extent of visual concern to a finite horizon.

One ends up with something that has the look of a big piece of wooden furniture, that does not look much like a building, or perhaps changes our perception of what a building is. The *double entendre* is embodied in questions of an enlarged model and scale, hence the issues of size and monumentality.

Ben Ami Shulman before 1935

6 MENDELSOHN STREET

Mendelsohn Street, a quiet road in the north of Tel Aviv with some successful buildings, belongs to the Geddes conceptual plan, done in the 1920s. Although the residential roads are situated between busy commercial streets, they are planned almost as a maze, discouraging drivers using them as short cuts.

The street leading to No. 6 provides a good view of its bulk and elevation. The building stands on round columns or pilotis, proportioned to emphasise the shaded entrance hall, which has well-handled details.

The main statement lies in the strong composition of the front elevation, where the style is freely handled. Three balconies on the left are semicircular in plan, but stuck on a smooth, plain surface. A line is effectively run vertically up to the roof, rising from the horizontal line of the extended balcony on the first floor. It is also followed by the flower container, cast in concrete.

The more surprising gesture is the roof pergola – a rounded projection, raised on a round pillar. This helps the sculptural, half-transparent completion of the statement above the horizontal roofline. Few buildings in the narrow streets in Tel Aviv are seen from a distance. This one is a good example of the development of the full potential of the Bauhaus style.

Gershon Stempler 1937

11 NIZANA STREET, JAFFA

The fact that the building is equipped with slatted wood blinds and has a pronounced opulence of form reveals it to be in a different vein to the usual Tel Aviv Bauhaus blend. These slight departures characterise the local Arab version, brought from Europe by way of the influence of the British Mandate. The International Style has a different interpretation in Jaffa, chiefly marked by its less austere features. There are not many examples and this is one of the few well-preserved ones, mainly because it was originally soundly built.

A residential building with three entrances, each leading to two apartments, it has the necessary preparations for upper storeys to be added – the usual practice in Jaffa. A further local anomaly is the use of stone, well-liked by Arab people but seldom employed in Bauhaus designs. The presence of the ground-floor shops is lively, creating a diversity which is appropriate to the small and well-proportioned public square in which the building is placed.

In fact, here one can see the interaction of architecture, design and the formation of a unique urban space, something that is only rarely a product of the International Style.

David Tlil 1936

35 PETAH TIQWA ROAD

Unique in its unfailing repetitiveness, this composition makes a striking and lasting impression. It is situated on the borders of the east-central part of Tel Aviv, on a major inter-city road leading to the north and close to the central bus and train stations. The commercial nature of the area dictates a ground floor of shops and other retail functions.

The geometry develops from a straight line on a diagonal plane, combining the elevation of the shops with a continuous wave of balustrades.

The International Style had not developed an architectural system based on repetitions, modules, regularity of elements, etc. Instead, forms were derived from a free vocabulary, with some personal, expressionist and even monumental elements. The building we see here develops a repetitive geometry on the first and higher floors, at 45 degrees to the original street line and the ground floor and aligned with the border of the site. This achieves a new orientation, slightly isolated from a busy road. Normally sharp corners are rounded to soften the effect. The modular approach, new for its time, is then used along the full length of the façade. There are no further embellishments or ornamentation. The end of the row is simply blocked off.

Shlomo Liaskovski and Jacob Orenstein 1935

Kawasaki
SANYANG
אבי הונדה

12 PINSKER STREET

A corner composition by the famous architect and town planner Richard Kaufman, one of the forerunners of the International Movement in Palestine.

Two cubes are opposed to each other: one has shaded balconies, the other uses the cantilevered protection of the windows as shading, a cubist idea realised with fine proportions. Horizontal strips are the mark of the style, and here they are used functionally to protect and to shade. The depth of the cube is enhanced and the composition becomes enticing and surprising at the fully exposed corner.

The solid mass of the original cube is not broken. This heaviness in the volume could have been more expressive or dynamic, but purity of expression, a valid aspiration at the time, hardly allows for that.

Richard Kaufman 1934

28 ROSH PINA STREET

This residential block on the corner of Ayelet Hashahar Street is situated in the extreme east of Tel Aviv, far from any centres of public activity, on land that would have been very cheap. It has a few neighbours built in the same style, which is curious as the surroundings have always been neglected. The area is deteriorating rapidly because of traffic and the proximity of industrial plants. All the buildings around stood on a sandstone hill, which was excavated when an approach to the central bus station became imperative – hence the tall retaining walls which place the buildings on a podium.

This is a very clear attempt at a stylistic exercise, and quite successful in a rough way, a little sketchy perhaps, but fully demonstrating the principles involved. There is more liveliness shown here and in neighbouring buildings than in the main bulk of Bauhaus building in the north of the city. Different colouring has been employed, and the local plan has a few geometrical peculiarities and odd angles in the original land division.

A simple shape on a raised platform, it is reminiscent of some early European Bauhaus designs and does not look particularly residential as the balconies do not play a significant role. However, the creation of a round corner, quite sharp in plan, is a dynamic strategy. The horizontal strips that meet the vertical shaft create some links to the volume to the right.

Arieh Cohen 1935

82 ROTHSCHILD BOULEVARD

The symmetry of this corner building is a drawback, especially in the context of the Bauhaus in Tel Aviv. The style does not favour such a formalist approach as it rarely serves the over-riding purpose of showing the vertical axis at its best. Furthermore, the cubist design approach which considers form in all its three-dimensionality cannot allow symmetry around an axis, which would be a contradiction in terms.

However, this building is striking because of its important position, and because of other Bauhaus characteristics such as the tall glass of the stairwell and the horizontal strips of windows and balconies. The element at the roof provides a finishing touch, and reaffirms the Bauhaus connection.

(Plan, see page 247.)

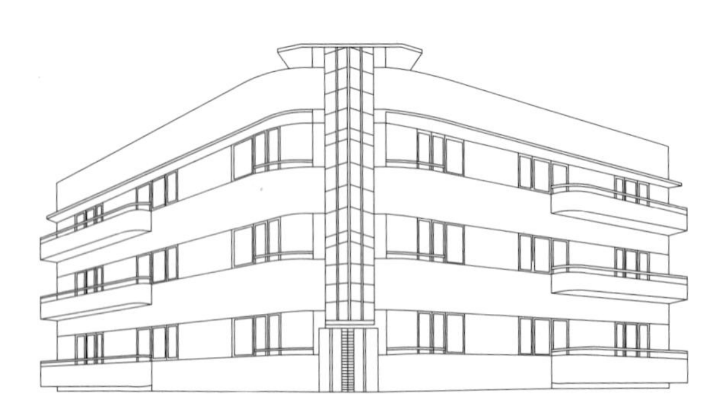

Joseph and Zeev Berlin 1932

82

84 ROTHSCHILD BOULEVARD

The story goes that this was the first building in Tel Aviv to be raised on freestanding columns, and thus the local forerunner of the International Style, with an early Bauhaus look. Today the building has been transformed beyond recognition by odd additions in various styles, including a malformed extension on the roof. The ground floor was barricaded in the 1948 war with a brick wall, still in place. The archive photograph opposite shows the unfortunate building in an earlier, uncompromised state.

The building is probably the best-known work by Jacob Rechter, a talented and pioneering architect. An important artistic achievement, it displays many design qualities. It is indeed a culmination of the expressionist qualities of the Bauhaus style. It is done with control, but it is the style that permits this sort of adventure.

A variety of elements are employed, and even when judged on their individual merits they are outstandingly successful because of a mixture of daring and originality. The unity of the composition, which can now only be appreciated in early photographs, is maintained.

The tension created through the positioning of the elements makes this building outstanding without theatricality, a danger inherent in any overtly expressionist design.

Jacob Rechter 1933

117 ROTHSCHILD BOULEVARD

A wider than usual block situated on Tel Aviv's main boulevard, a popular site during the Bauhaus period. Because of height restrictions and the double-sized corner plot, two entrance halls are used here. Symmetry has been avoided, and the positioning of the wings does not seem to be more restricted than normal.

The main interest here is in the recess formed to the street front. This is used for the garden, but it also enhances the corner and, in conjunction with the space of the boulevard, creates a bigger space. The central cube has its corners slightly rounded off, a treatment that is employed a little too often and sometimes reminds one of the Bauhaus furniture of the period. It can also add to the effect of a cardboard model.

Using a different colour for the two stairs volumes is unusual, but it is interesting enough, despite the theatrical effect and connotations. It is helped by the fenestration of the staircase.

Although the people living on Rothschild Boulevard, especially this northern part, are wealthier than the average, the upkeep of the place is not as good as one might hope, as the paint and some of the stucco have deteriorated. It proved to be very difficult to build soundly with the concrete blocks available in the 1930s, tied by the questionable method of sparse reinforced-concrete columns and beams. Inevitably, expansion forces have caused minor cracks to appear, cracks that could not be repaired, spoiling the stucco and any paint applied, especially synthetic-based paints.

Ytzhak Rapoport 1933

142 ROTHSCHILD BOULEVARD

A very sensitive and subdued composition in spite, or perhaps because, of a very central and conspicuous site, opposite the Habima National Theatre. Using the whole of a big parcel of land in a good urban position, this is an ample block that deploys the Bauhaus style fully. Standing on the quiet side of a square, the building actually starts on the adjacent boulevard. It appears to float, resting on a raised basement floor.

The originality and quality of the design rest with the cantilevered balconies and the details of the rounded balustrades. They form an airy addition to a simple form with fine openings, simply proportioned.

Some changes occurred when the building was restored a few years ago – in particular, one of the principal entries was altered and blocked off.

(Plan, see page 250.)

Dov Carmi 1935/renovation Ytzhak Iashar and Aliza Toledo 1999

7 RUPIN STREET

Some of Tel Aviv's important Bauhaus-period buildings are in too poor a state to be shown and we may have to wait for some years before they are restored. But the process of raising public interest in the city as a treasury of the Bauhaus and the International Style has started. Architecture, as a form of art, has to be taken care of continuously. Furthermore, it is apparent that architecture ages well when it has been designed well.

The composition at 7 Rupin Street is striking and very original in many respects. It also contains some features that are not usually found in Bauhaus design, and it is important to note that one of the characteristics of the period is the presence of expressionist elements. This tendency carries basic Bauhaus ideas a little further through the artistic freedom inherent in it and the possibility it provided for sculptural three-dimensional development. Here the walls, acting as extended balustrades, are freely shaped as non-functional elements, but tied into the extended proportions which are controlled by the strip windows. In the recessed second block, the walls are again freestanding, true to the cubist feeling of the whole. The two basic cubes are also well articulated in the usual Bauhaus vein, and display original and playful invention.

The addition of the roof as a functional garden and leisure feature and the free-standing first floor raised on pilotis both help to generate a sense of freedom in the new, communal residential building.

The drawbacks of the style are also here, with the cardboard-model look of a building that is somehow too good to be true, almost a symbolic illustration of a new habitat for 'modern man'.

(Plan, see page 251.)

Mitelman & Milbauer c 1936

12 RUPIN STREET

The main success in this original composition lies in the principal elevation, in the success of achieving much-sought transparency or lightening of the mass through its many pierced volumes and flat planes. Added to that is a profusion of balconies, the chief sign of urbanity in a residential building. Their strength here is in their accumulation as a broken frontal wall, giving residents a space in which to sunbathe. Thus this block looks designed explicitly for the well-being of its middle-class occupants.

The block also achieves complexity in a style noted for its striving for simplicity. It is an illustration of the fact that personal expression will play its part in design, sometimes extending the limits of a style. The symmetry looks almost inevitable.

The notion of well-being is inseparable from the International Style, and it may even be stated to be its *raison d'etre*. This is sadly lacking in its aftermath during the post-war period of easy, do-it-yourself modernity that left us with the cheap repetitive apartment block. They often became unventilated slum dwellings, refuges for the poor, and enclosures of social problems.

Shmuel Mistechkin 1938

65 SHENKIN STREET

Lucian Korngold was active in Tel Aviv in 1933–35, before returning to Warsaw. By 1940 he had moved to San Paolo, where he became well-known.

An impressive corner building in the centre of the city, his design for 65 Shenkin Street is more than usually intricate for the period. It looks modern even today, almost 70 years after its conception, and the block plays an important role in the local street pattern.

The main volume turns well and connects into interesting horizontally shaded balconies, which are skilfully detailed. The material is a washed stucco in multi-coloured pebbles. The pronounced round windows included in the design were to become a popular and widespread motif. Some decorative accents are visible in the rainwater spouts, adding charm to the precise overall geometry.

Ground floor and entrance constitute an innovative feature for the period, known as the 'house on stilts'. This was to become a local landmark of the style, controversial for a while but finally widely accepted. It has, of course, numerous international counterparts. Proportions are well studied and realised, and the roof has been maintained as a useable space, another modern innovation but related to Middle-Eastern tradition.

The design can be understood as an example of a moderately free plan and an expressive elevation, both the outcome of the use of reinforced-concrete construction. The wall becomes a modulated surface while the surrounding external space is shaped by the exclusion of one corner of the mass.

This is fine example of its period and one which has been the subject of genuine public attention, especially in terms of conservation.

Lucian Korngold 1935

12 SHLOMO HAMELEH STREET

Shlomo Hamelech Street has a number of buildings in the Bauhaus style, built between 1930 and 1940. Once modestly elegant, it is past its heyday, but the number of well-designed buildings in the same style and to the same scale is unique; the modernity and the collective look of this street can be cited as a kind of historical event.

No. 12 is an example of an unfortunate symmetrical approach, rarely chosen on theoretical grounds as well as on grounds of suitability. It could have worked, because the site is on a corner, but the fact does not help here. The building looks as though it were intended for a larger site. The composition opts for an exaggerated monumentality on its corner, but it looks uncalled for, especially the emphatic accents of the grilled opening at the very top. The raised cantilever used for shading helps the composition.

Detailing is logical and well done. The balustrades contribute to the effect of the whole. The placing of the protective cantilevers on a lower level than the floors introduces interesting proportions in the composition of the corner.

Pinhas Hutt and I Klugerman 1935

6209061

27 SHLOMO HAMELEH STREET

A simple, original and clear design, still looking interesting after almost 70 years. The quality of its execution has been matched by the high performance of materials and detailing. Because of this the building has been reasonably easy to maintain over a long period.

Its originality lies in the seemingly effortlessly placed balustrade, a quasi-wall, serving also as a brise-soleil. The balcony abruptly changes into a completely different one, on the same floor level, with some originally detailed horizontal steel bars, formed into a semicircle in plan. Looking at this fine example of the components and basic impulses behind the Bauhaus, the principles become clearer.

When the architect combines a knack of using new technologies with an elegant treatment of new forms, the quality of the design reaches beyond the period of its construction. The lines of the design have their roots in the machine age and the eloquence of Le Corbusier, and can be seen as the gentle precursors of Japanese architecture of the mid and late twentieth century, with its abrupt brutalism and cool postmodern attitude.

Yehuda Fogel and Shlomo Mekori 1936

3 YAEL STREET

An outstanding three-dimensional corner composition made in two consecutive steps in opposition to each other. This is where its success lies: it speaks in two voices. The base or podium, unexpected in a modern composition, is one and a half storeys tall. It is very freely formed, with a round shaded entrance, semi-dark and inviting, flanked by two symmetrical open stairs leading to the first-storey elevated garden. These stairs still appear clearly modern. Their flatly worked out shapes are a reminder of Russian constructivist graphics and they have a pronounced precise geometrical flair. Precision is enhanced by a steel balustrade to the stair, carefully and minimally executed. The little gate has imaginative features, and the steel has a high-tech look for its period. It is effective in its severity and rigid ornamentation.

The main bulk of the structure is positioned on top of this pedestal. It is a simple and contrasting block, rectangular and with the same quality of precision. Rows of balconies in front lighten the composition and a pergola on the roof adds some transparency to that contributed by the one on the first-floor recess. This lightness is not often found.

Like its neighbour at 5 Yael Street, the approach here combines originality and know-how. The result is one of Tel Aviv's best buildings in the International Style. Details in this building are of a special quality, and are truly inventive. They are looked at on pages 232 and 233.

Oskar Kaufman 1935

5 YAEL STREET

The success of this elevation – the only view one gets of this building from this side street – derives from the variation of surfaces, and this is achieved by the treatment of the balustrades. It should be read in conjunction with the elevation on 27 Shlomo Hamelech Street. Brown ceramic tiles at both entrances add a welcome touch of colour. Two round windows of the porthole type adorn the entry doors. Off-white pebble-textured stucco provides relief from the usual glare of white surfaces. The finish is of the best quality, and as it emulates chemically a cement concrete composition (it is in fact almost a bare concrete finish) it is very resistant to the climate.

The principal balustrade is broken off vertically from the secondary one. It is almost a completely solid wall, with the vertical surface of the brise soleil hanging down a considerable distance. Horizontal slits mark the repetition of the floors. The next balcony has a totally different balustrade, a steel mesh, transparent and decorative. This sort of inventive and courageous treatment distinguishes good Bauhaus design from the average.

Yehuda Fogel and Shlomo Mekori 1936

PUBLIC BUILDINGS

56 ALLENBY STREET

A simple well-proportioned cube with a very subdued corner treatment, the indentations on the elevations and the cubist balcony mark this building as belonging to the International Style. The identical elevations on all sides are an uncommon feature, and could be criticised as providing an easy way out for the architect. The other feature which is striking is the modular and repetitive window, the same all over the building. This is the product of an attitude that developed again in architecture from the early 1950s and has survived to the present day.

A recent renovation added a new floor behind a tall brown balustrade The extension succeeds because it does not play in opposition to the Bauhaus aesthetic. It is distinctive and more courageous than the original composition.

Joseph Merrer and Lotte Cohen 1936/renovated 2001

אלנבי
IVECO

4 BELINSON STREET
THEATRE HAOEL

The Theatre Haoel used to be a popular hall for a company financed and supported by the workers' movement. Now empty and awaiting renovation, it had a reputation for the quality of its repertoire throughout its 60-year existence.

In combination with the building slightly to its north, the slight curve and the height of the building help to form a secondary, much reduced public square hidden away behind the more prominent Dizengof Square. Not much of the Bauhaus vocabulary has been used, apart from the row of openings forming a two-storey internal balcony. The only vestiges to be seen are their projection to the front of the elevation. Nevertheless, there is an imposing presence to the theatre and the slightly earlier building at 14 Ben Ami Street, an affinity in their heights and appearance, almost a common urban attitude.

Arieh Sharon 1939

14 BEN AMI STREET

Similarity with the theatre by Arieh Sharon a little further down the street (see page 118), turns the two buildings into a partnership which achieves a common space-forming coherence, not often found. While this kind of cooperation between architects and buildings is rare, when it occurs it proves the importance of this sharing of public roles in defining space.

The horizontal lines and gentle curve are the chief Bauhaus features here, with the effect of the shaded balconies. These give the building a light and friendly look, without obscuring its magnitude, which conveys a certain monumentality.

14 Ben Ami Street and Theatre Haoel form the boundary of a centrally located residential neighbourhood. The abrupt change in scale here has the surprising and inappropriate look of a quickly planned new town, with no attempt to manage the transitions.

Joseph Noifeld 1937

75 BEN GURION BOULEVARD

The building occupies a very central site on a corner with Adam Hacohen Street in the northern part of Tel Aviv. Despite its location, it was empty for many years. Owned and used as a meeting place by the leftist wings of the Mapaï workers party, it was surrounded by a big agricultural plot (a sign of the belief in the value of communal urban gardens), and some youth-movement clubs. These were built over in the 1980s, and the original building was restored by the Tel Aviv municipality in 1992–93 to something very close to its original shape. Some new functions (a club and a restaurant) were included, and the front garden was turned into a terrace. Unfortunately, in 1995 a suicide bomber killed and wounded many users. Normal functions are now suspended.

A well-proportioned, well-turned three-dimensional design, the building is a pleasure to look at, even though in the harsh sunshine the flat stucco produces a white glare – a disadvantage in this and other similar designs. Nevertheless, it is a friendly composition, using a colonnaded setback and an inviting entrance with a big plate-glass window shaded by an overhang. The ground floor is a happier design than the floor above. The motif of the colonnade is carried above by an impressive and well-balanced pergola. These broken surfaces are a good example of the way practitioners of the style could achieve transparency in the mass of a building.

The chief drawbacks of the Bauhaus approach are clear here: the detailing does not withstand Tel Aviv's climate very long or very well. Expensive new methods are needed to prolong the lives of these buildings beyond a 30-year limit.

Finkerfeld 1934

DIZENGOF SQUARE

1 ZAMENHOF STREET/89 DIZENGOF STREET

The design of a large public square (100 metres in diameter) in the middle of the twentieth century using a very modern approach is unique. Dizengof Square is still the symbol of Tel Aviv, and it is also the chief exhibit of the prevailing style of its time. It was the result of a public design competition won by Genia Averbuch, then a young architect.

The principal idea of rounded forms and balconies looks like a happy solution, but the shape imposed limitations on the buildings because of the technology available at the time. Fibre-reinforced concrete might have provided an easier solution, especially for the hung projections of the balconies. These brise soleils are done in plastered wire mesh which inevitably rusts. Not all the balconies are useable; some are decorative.

The circular space created here formed a good public meeting place, and remained so for decades. In the 1970s the traffic conditions became too harsh, and this led to an unfortunate and hasty alteration. Changing the original traffic lanes, bringing them underground, brought even more traffic. Public activity was allocated to a new, upper deck, but the feeling of the urban space was wrecked, and people finally moved elsewhere, to Rabin Square.

Today, the place is virtually abandoned, despite lots of effort, both commercial and municipal. The traffic is hard to negotiate, and sun, weather and fumes are unpleasant, as are the harsh concrete surfaces. The central Agam sculpture only aggravates the problems of the space because of its uncalled for size.

Recent renovation has brought to the fore the attractive features of the design of the square, and it can be appreciated again. There is some thought of reverting to the original design with a roundabout as a means of controlling traffic, but this plan remains doubtful.

Genia Averbuch 1940

1 ZAMENHOF STREET

YEHUDA MEGIDOVITZ 1939

1 ZAMENHOF STREET

YEHUDA MEGIDOVITZ 1939

89 DIZENGOF STREET

GENIA AVERBUCH 1940/RENOVATED 2001

31 GROUSENBERG STREET

A small example of the style going through one of its preferred motions, rounding a corner. The environment is a busy commercial district and it is a minor wonder that the building is well-preserved. The design is precise; its performance has been managed in the formative horizontal lines. The presence of the architect's tool, the T-square on the drawing board, can be felt very strongly.

It is one of the smallest examples to survive, and is well sited on its corner. Its rarity is enhanced by its off-pink colour.

Ben Ami Shulman 1939

31

60 JABOTINSKY STREET
ASSUTA HOSPITAL

The successes of this privately owned hospital are manifold. It is situated in a busy part of northern Tel Aviv, but hidden away so as limit the effects of noise. It has been planned on an attractive human scale (a feature hard to find in modern clinics and hospitals); it has a pleasant appearance of modernity, and is sited in a good-sized garden.

The simplicity of the design is misleading. It is in fact a complex composition, which appears from all sides as a clean, perhaps rather antiseptic but well-detailed example of the potential of the Bauhaus style. The building demands respect for its successful austerity and quality of execution. Geometry and proportions are always precise and unrelenting. The building has been modified and refurbished many times but has never lost its original freshness and charm. It is now somewhat hidden from the street, but its internal spaces are worth visiting, even though they are somewhat divorced from the surrounding life of the city.

The architectural details are very modestly done and their simplicity helps them to appear friendly. The building looks more like a clinic than a hospital, and it has happily been kept to its original size.

Joseph Noifeld 1934

62

37 LILIENBLUM STREET

A fully urban example of International Style design. No garden or tree embellishes this heavy block which has survived because it was used as a banking office from the start. Its full use of the site, encroaching on to the pavement, is a sign of the drawbacks of the system; it looks very much like a model of itself. It does not fit well into the townscape and is fairly anonymous.

The corner is taken in a standard way but the well-protected strip windows are monotonous, being badly proportioned and heavy-handed, especially as they do not change height or width with the progress of the elevation.

The only originality is in the round canopy to the side entrance with its recess and tall winged detail, which looks like a logo or sign.

Dov Kozinsky 1937

MAGEN DAVID SQUARE

This irregular, oddly shaped space is formed by six corner buildings, a few of which are prominent because of their Bauhaus features. They are of mixed use and Magen David Square is a central business thoroughfare – all the streets leading to it are primarily commercial. There are good connections south to Jaffa and north and west to other squares. It was one of Tel Aviv's first public squares, and here the local grids change into the dominant urban pattern – a north–south alignment. It is interesting to note that the grids coming from Jaffa are radial and they have to swing into the more modern, north–south grid.

The design shared by the corner buildings makes this a modern landmark – a rounded plan, no garden or involved play of masses, and greater height than most structures in the area. On top, they are marked by a pergola, a concrete column-and-beam structure serving nominally as a shade-forming garden element, but never used as such. Two of the buildings carry the mark of the local Bauhaus style very prominently. There is even a degree of monumentality.

Heavy traffic, especially public transport, makes this square useless for any communal function. Nevertheless, it is easily recognisable as a prominent urban feature.

Yehuda Megidovitz 1938 (left)/Shlomo Liaskovski, Jacob Orenstein 1934 (right)

13 MAZEH STREET
MAGEN DAVID HOUSE

A clinic, this is one of the few fully public buildings in the Bauhaus style, and was designed by the department of public works in the Tel Aviv municipality. Its form appears very simplified, without any recognisable design or decorative elements. It is in fact a significant but unsuccessful work unusual in the barrenness of its forms, and eloquent in revealing much of the weakness of a style.

The design is based on a few volumes, open and recessed balconies, plus a functional garage for ambulances. It seems that the architect could not find a way around the bare functionalist approach. A composition has been started but it does not unfold and stops short of offering a decisive statement. The small site does not allow a cubist form to develop, but this is clearly what the composition is about.

Jacob Ben Sira (Town Architect) 1934

56 MAZEH STREET
HAARETZ PRINT WORKS

The *Haaretz* newspaper is associated with the well-known Shoken family, and brings to mind the Shoken office building in Berlin, originally designed by Erich Mendelsohn (who later immigrated to Palestine).

A modestly dramatic front is presented to the small residential street. It is not clear how this machine-packed and potentially noisy print works was given permission to be built here. On the remaining empty half parcel a residential block was added at the end of the twentieth century. The original building was quite successfully refurbished to its original shape, and the print works, with the offices, moved to new quarters.

The building calls to mind other pure Bauhaus examples, including designs by the Bauhaus founder Walter Gropius, such as the Fagos factory (1914) and the Bauhaus School itself (1925). The free and lavish use of steel-framed glass is offset by strong, square stuccoed shapes. The severity is somewhat reduced by the rounded balcony, balustrade and cantilever roof, as well as the base of the stairwell volume. The effect is very clear, and is actually enhanced by the new coloured residential block behind it.

Joseph and Zeev Berlin 1934

2 PINSKER STREET

The material from which this office is built draws attention immediately. This is the local sandstone, very seldom, if ever, used in public or indeed any sizeable buildings. It has a soft appearance and is grey-yellow. However, here we are looking at an artificial variant, manufactured and used as cladding. It has weathered well.The local stone reacts very favourably to the humidity and sea wind, and has the advantage of a non-reflective surface. Old towns on the coast of Israel were traditionally built in it: Jaffa, Caesaria, Acre, to name just a few, are all sandstone. It contrasts strongly with the much stronger but monotonous off-white limestone whose reflecting surface produces a lot of glare.

The Bauhaus approach, with its associations with the machine age and manufactured materials, does not use natural stone. The mass of this building has a softened external appearance. The rounded shapes, especially at the southern corner, are the strongest evidence of the Bauhaus approach, supported by the first-floor strip window. An internal court is reached through a shaded short passage, the entrance to the whole.

This is the main building forming the public Mougrabi Square, leading to the sea, which gives it an important advantage in terms of its presence. The building also helps to point the way north to Dizengof Square.

Ytzhak Rapoport c 1935

BARRACUDA

8 RESH GALUTA STREET, JAFFA

A very unusual example of the Bauhaus mode in the township of Jaffa to the south of Tel Aviv. Ahmed Damiaty was not the only Arab architect to adopt the style, but very little is known of these modernist architects as a group. Nothing that can be said of the developing style in the new Jewish state applies here. At most the adoption of the Bauhaus style represents an isolated example of Western influence in the midst of the local vernacular, which is very differently oriented and involves different technologies and methods. It may be that the route of influence was through graduates of British architecture schools, as the regulating plans and the planning officers in Jaffa were British during the period of the Mandate.

Our building has the merits of size and an overall clarity of design and orientation. The influence of art-deco motifs can be discerned. Nearby – mainly along Yehuda Hayamit Street – are a few more examples in the same vein but of a lower standard.

Jaffa was deserted by most of its inhabitants in 1948, during the war, and so was this building. Its lower, mainly commercial, floor was totally unused for 40 years. It was renovated and refurbished in the 1990s when it was turned into a senior citizens' social club.

The plan occupies one whole block, an irregularly shaped parcel which is used well and fully, with rounding of the corners. The whole residential floor is ventilated by one central court. The round motif is repeated in walls, balustrades, and other more purely decorative elements.

(Plan, see page 246.)

Ahmed Damiaty 1936

19 ROTHSCHILD BOULEVARD

One of the few large-scale, non-residential, imposing buildings done in the wake of the Bauhaus. Its situation – on a major boulevard and on a prominent corner – has of course influenced its status.

The lower storeys, close to the busy street, are better done than those above. Their articulation is vivid and pronounced, as well as being inventive. The store fronts with their glazed openings are lightweight. The two top storeys may look like a later addition, but they are not. The rounded principal corner does not end with any effect or attempt at forming a balustrade or architrave.

The recessed balconies are an important statement, both because they provide shade from the glare of the sun and because they have a pronounced impact on the way we read the building. The balcony has the effect of announcing the notion of leisure, symbolically beneficial to the appearance of the structure.

This building is a reminder of the curious and unfortunate fact that architectural concerns tend to lessen the further up a building we go. Indeed, the first three storeys deal well with the corner and contribute to the street in a significant way. The rest of the building is disappointing in its standard shape.

Zaki Chelouche 1937

RUTH SQUARE PAVILION

There are two pavilions in Ruth Square. One serves as a kiosk, a building selling soft drinks. These used to be a common feature in squares and boulevards in Tel Aviv, well-suited to the climate and a more leisurely way of life. Being sited on public property, most have now been demolished. The other small pavilion (pictured opposite), around 5 metres square, houses an electricity transformer.

Both look as though they were designed by the same hand, in the Bauhaus style. The electricity substation has been well maintained, and retains all the original functional openings, ventilating grill included. The form has artistic connotations, with rounded projections and cantilevers, and these turn it into a naive example of the style, a little timid perhaps, but nonetheless exemplary.

architect and date unknown

2 STRAUSS STREET

BALFOUR PRIMARY SCHOOL

Not many of Tel Aviv's public buildings were designed in the International Style, chiefly because money was scarce during the Bauhaus period and it was uncertain how many people were going to live in the new town. The Balfour Primary School is mainly a purist composition of cubic masses representing the basic tradition of the Bauhaus style. In the year it was built, 1935, it would have been seen as a pioneering structure (for a similar public building see 195 Ben Yehuda Street). It was designed in the town hall's architectural department, a rare strategy for that period. The main entrance, the somewhat ornamental balustrade above it, the thin wall on the right with a big squared grille cut into it, the towering striped stairwell with the clock, all remind one of contemporary European examples of the style. Less successful are the south-facing windows which are slightly undecided in their proportions.

The schoolyard (internal and not too large) is not integrated in the composition; this often happens with public designs and is still a common fault. It is also clear that the building is not well exposed to the street, nor does it create an external public space.

Proponents of the International Style were seldom concerned with urban problems or urban theory. Their main interest rested with the end product, the building and its appearance. This sometimes resulted in a faceless architecture, at best somewhat theatrical or theoretical in its cleanliness, to the point where buildings may have the look of cardboard models. It was left to the more imaginative architects to make expressive and personal statements, but even then the urban role of many buildings leaves a lot to be desired, especially in the formation of public space.

Comparison with the archive photograph on pages 150–151 shows a few changes to the original building.

Jacob Ben Sira and S Shifman 1935

PUBLIC BUILDINGS

3 STRAUSS STREET
TEACHERS' ASSOCIATION HEADQUARTERS

A very effective and subdued composition, formalist and interested only in the proportions of an elevation. It is in fact the product of a purist approach, which has nothing to do with any functionality, orientation or symbolic meaning. Yet there is a true dynamic feeling in this façade, even a relationship with the street, and the clean treatment is unusual. It was built in stages and completed rather late in terms of the style. Nevertheless the mark of the Bauhaus is there, in the true flat positioning of the elements.

Zvi Dgani 1950

בית המורה

NEW AND RENEWED BUILDINGS

21 BIALIK STREET

The International Style has characteristics whose purity and severity may lend a structure the look of a public building even when its use is private – as here. The window proportions and their divisions are over-emphatic, and one thinks of a public building such as a school, developed at a later period. These windows would introduce the light needed in a classroom but are superfluous in a private residence, especially here in the East.

The building originally comprised six dwellings, each with three or four rooms. Abandoned in the 1950s, it was in urgent need of repair when it was rented out to become a dental clinic. As it stands on the old municipal square, opposite Tel Aviv's first town hall, it served as municipal offices for many years, during which it deteriorated completely and was finally deserted. Between 1985 and 2000 it was a ruin. Then municipal plans were made that involved trying to refurbish a few buildings on Bialik Street – private as well as public – and it acquired more value.

The new owners of the property were persuaded to devote part of the ground floor to a museum for a private collection of Bauhaus furniture, and a keeper's flat was included. The remaining two floors became two spacious flats, the top one with a studio on the roof, a roof garden, and a new lift.

The premises were completely renovated, with the proviso that most of the elevations were to revert to their original appearance. Establishing what this had been had to include some guesswork because, as is usually the case, changes had occurred very early on. Some structural mistakes, such as columns which go through the cantilevered balconies, had to remain, so as to be true to the original building. Apart from that, most of the external details were kept and completely renewed, along with the original internal stairway. Specially imported hydrated lime plaster on a reinforced-steel mesh was used, as the original walls were very poor quality and completely out of true.

Shmuel Gipstein 1935/renovation Nahoum Cohen and Boubi Luxemburg 2000

69 DIZENGOF STREET

A newly built block of flats, on a long-neglected central site. The size of the plot is close to 900 square metres, and the built floor area is accordingly large, up to 3000 square metres. This is a big undertaking by local standards, especially in this prime location. The new block has preserved, respected and enhanced the public space at street level. New local by-laws state that the floors of uncovered balconies do not count as rateable space: hence the cantilevered and bottomless projections which serve as brise-soleils.

Bauhaus memories feature strongly in the design of the block, witness to the influence that still lingers. Among the reasons for this are the ease of execution the style offers and its ready acceptance locally. The block lacks any originality or display of special talent; the designer has not even tried to lessen the oppressive effect of its bulk. Nevertheless, its solidity and relative simplicity is welcome in a city suffering simultaneously from a rapid deterioration of quality and much over-design.

This building can be compared with its neighbour to the south, a large block housing families turned off the land now occupied by the big commercial centre on the same street. It is an atrocious undertaking, and has been in a very bad state since it was built.

Elisha Rubin 2001

Tal Bagels

166 DIZENGOF STREET

When buildings are extended vertically, it is has become usual practice not to respect the original design, even when it is publicly recognised as part of the city's Bauhaus heritage, and even when it is very clearly a good and well-executed example. Changing the design after a certain height is an aspect of the Israeli disregard for rules or common understanding, to the point where disrespect is shown as matter of principle. And of course this can be very pronounced when we are facing the city's large, central, and very obvious Bauhaus heritage. Excuses can be very sophisticated and Talmudic. Apparently, the old is more respected by overlaying it with a completely personal and utterly different approach than by adhering to the principles of the original. However, a survey of the present state of Bauhaus buildings fails to uncover a good example of this approach.

Here, the fact that the location is very public makes the issue even more open to debate. It is clear to an onlooker that something strange has taken place, and the two pieces of design, forced to cohabit on the street corner, are still unsettled.

The sculptural effect achieved is still architectural and not overdone, even when there is no sharing of elements, say of balconies and balustrades. The presence of the building is sober and calculated, and maybe that saves it.

A Mitelman 1936/Pinhas Doron 1995

shu uemura

2 HARAV FRENKEL STREET

The district of Florentin, to the south of Tel Aviv near Jaffa, went through revival and renewal in the 1990s. This is the densest residential district in Israel and it was poorly built by absentee landlords as a development for rent, an unusual practice here. The poverty of the residents, the high population density and the smallness of the flats all contributed to the creation of a slum. Recent growth in incomes has permitted some improvement of conditions, in which the author of this book took part as a town planning chief advisor.

The block of flats at 2 Harav Frenkel Street has two entrances, and used to have three floors with some mixed uses, which can be detrimental to the renewal of a building. The new construction was done by the owners, and had to take place while the then residents were still in place. Thus all the new floors had to span the whole existing building. A system of columns had to be placed on the external walls, with new and deeper foundations – an extremely complex undertaking. The local code permits extensive building rights, carried over from the original utterly unscrupulous over-use of building ratios, almost to the point where densities reached dangerous levels. However, the original design was respected, and a fact that helped was that the district carries overtones of the Bauhaus in almost every building.

It may seem inevitable that the addition would mean that the building's proportions would become heavy and burdensome. It turned out that the corner site, with its setback allowing space for a small public square, was beneficial. With the balconies, this allowed the elevation to be opened up.

Y Borenstein 1933/restoration and addition Nahoum Cohen 1997

14 PEKIIN STREET

A new single-family residence in the north-central part of Tel Aviv. The site is a street corner adjoining a public garden, part of the Geddes Plan which laid out quiet, bending and difficult-to-navigate residential streets around small public gardens, a form repeated in the areas adjoining the local south-to-north commercial streets.

The original building, which dates from around 1940, contained five small flats. It was not designed in a particular style, but had one balcony to the front reminiscent of simple, rounded Bauhaus shapes. The lines of this balcony helped the architects – who bought the old building in order to turn it into their own home – to establish an important link to the not-so-distant Bauhaus past of Tel Aviv.

The public stairway and much of the original external frame remained essentially intact. The opportunity was taken to put some meaning into the simple, nondescript original and turn it, subtly and paying homage to the architecture with which so many Israeli architects grew up, into something that is now almost a landmark. Executed with reserved elegance, the attempt is very successful, helped by good proportions and simple finishes.

Some of the side windows have been treated with freedom, adding a measure of late-modernist flair. The other windows are more conventionally placed. Flat roofs are put into use and internal courts are reformed, as the Tel Aviv weather demands.

It is not often that a building acknowledges freely and unselfconsciously an architect's debt to local design history. This building represents both a fresh design and a well-thought-through reference to the past.

Braha and Michael Chyutin 2000

22 PINSKER STREET

A very carefully executed three-floor addition. Scale and presence can be lacking in local architecture, and a bigger than average site offers an opportunity this building exploits effectively. It comprises 12 good-sized apartments, including three rooftop extensions which have the use of the roof on the next level. The new balconies are well-shaped, with the slits characteristic of the style but originally omitted. The building had some underground space, which has been used in the modern version for the vital car-parking. Notice the unusual total lack of garden or free space, the result of a local planning ruling.

The decision not to change the original forms and motifs was a wise one, and the full potential of the International Style has been exploited. Korngold's building does not show any sign of invention, but it is still an exemplary piece of design. In many similar cases of renovation and extension the original style has been compromised to allow the architects to display their originality. It is seldom beneficial.

Lucian Korngold 1935/addition 1999

104 ROTHSCHILD BOULEVARD

A good example of how closely some Bauhaus designers approached the aspirations of the art-deco movement in architecture. While art deco is a precursor of the Bauhaus style, as its name implies it was never much more than a decorative movement. Bauhaus practice had larger aims, and it emerged after a war that helped to shatter some of the more naive beliefs and that lead to some truly revolutionary thinking. But the precursor inevitably left its mark, especially in the elaboration of motifs.

The building on the corner of Rothschild Boulevard and Shenkin Street was expensively renovated in the last years of the 20th century. Changed from its original residential role to offices, it is still unoccupied. The change of use required a number of parking spaces, and by an enormous effort the whole structure was underpinned on steel sections, while a new underground garage was excavated. The extension which was built after additional building rights were granted looks flimsy, bleak and inconsequential. It ignores the style of the original, and does not attempt to make any particular statement.

The original building, while related to the prevailing Bauhaus tendency in combining the simple cube with some rounded cylinder shapes, seems overly ornate, particularly in the entrance and stairwell. The motif of three windows mirrors the mounting steps and is echoed by a similarly shaped protective overhang. This is the familiar zig-zag line of design which can be seen on many dinner and coffee sets of the period. The frontal symmetry is definitely odd, even for art deco. Nevertheless, while very few buildings deserve to be called truly interesting, this is one of them.

(Plan, see page 248.)

Yehuda Megidovitz 1937/renovated 1999

118 ROTHSCHILD BOULEVARD

A small renovated residential block facing Rothschild Boulevard. The work, in which the balconies were completely redone, has been very carefully executed. The balustrades are completely new, properly detailed to Bauhaus standards. All the Bauhaus elements are present, and with an almost postcard veracity. The full use of orthogonal design can be seen here – an attribute of the Bauhaus method. A creative imagination is very clear in the 'ladder' of the vertical window to the stairs, and in the proportion of the roof garden with its upper, concrete 'handle'. The twin window to the boulevard and the strip turning the corner at the balcony are further elements that are often encountered.

(Plan, see page 249.)

Ytzhak Rapoport 1935/renovated 1999

4 TARSAT BOULEVARD

An unusual and late take on the pergola as shading device appears in this protected public garden near the Habima National Theatre and the Mann Auditorium (both of which show the influence of the International Style). Trees normally provide all the shade in public gardens. In Tel Aviv this can be insufficient because of the strong sun and humidity. The public space here was raised to catch more of the westerly breezes and artificially shaded to create a very welcoming environment. The design fits well into the local design patterns and buildings. Being in a very central position, it also encompasses a few shops which encourage the public to use the space.

The well-kept gardens are situated in a district with many Bauhaus buildings. A good link between Rothschild and the Hen Boulevards, it is a useful urban element, not just a pleasant one.

Jacob Rechter 1965

Marcolin

DETAIL

ROOF GARDENS

14 GEORGE ELIOT STREET

BENJAMIN ANECKSTEIN c 1935

THE DETAILS OF THE ROOF PERGOLA AT 14 GEORGE ELIOT STREET ARE SHOWN IN AN ARCHIVE PHOTO. IT SHOWS HOW FRESH AND EXCITING THE BEAMS AND COLUMNS APPEARED SOON AFTER THEY WERE MADE. IT CERTAINLY LOOKS LIKE A MAJOR EFFORT, AND ONE CAN GUESS AT THE HOPE THAT WAS INVESTED IN THE PUBLIC ROLE OF THE ROOF GARDEN. UNFORTUNATELY, REALITY WAS HARSHER, AND THE CLIMATE DISCOURAGED MUCH USE. EXPECTATIONS OF THE ROOF GARDEN'S SOCIAL FUNCTION AS A PLACE WHERE NEIGHBOURS WOULD JOIN IN THE JOY OF COMMON PROPERTY, WERE TOO OPTIMISTIC. THE RESIDENTS, COMING FROM DIFFERENT BACKGROUNDS AND UNUSED TO THIS NEW MIDDLE-EASTERN WAY OF LIFE, DID NOT COOPERATE. THE ROOF GARDENS ARE NOW IN POOR CONDITION .

ROOF GARDENS

A protective garden trellis, its beams and columns producing shadow, and sometimes covered by climbing vegetation, is known as a pergola. It is a characteristic feature of buildings all around the Mediterranean, demanded by the climate and the degree to which life takes place outdoors, and it is still employed, mainly in residential and vernacular architecture.

Its Bauhaus connotations perhaps derive from the practice of Le Corbusier, a great admirer of Southern-European architectural elements. In his early villas (such as the Villa Savoye and Villa Stein) roof-garden features are incorporated in a modernist context. Many Tel Aviv architects admired and some even worked with Le Corbusier. Local conditions were perfect for life in the open, and the new ideals of communality and sharing were espoused by many architects and clients alike.

The time was ripe to incorporate this new element, which also has great possibilities for finishing off a composition with a freestanding sculptural structure. This ties in well with the concrete column, the piloti (which also has Corbusian connotations). The visual connection is in the creation of two free open spaces, protected and cultivated. The ground-floor columns and the top beam-and-column structure frame the main bulk of the building between them, and provide an additional sense of communality.

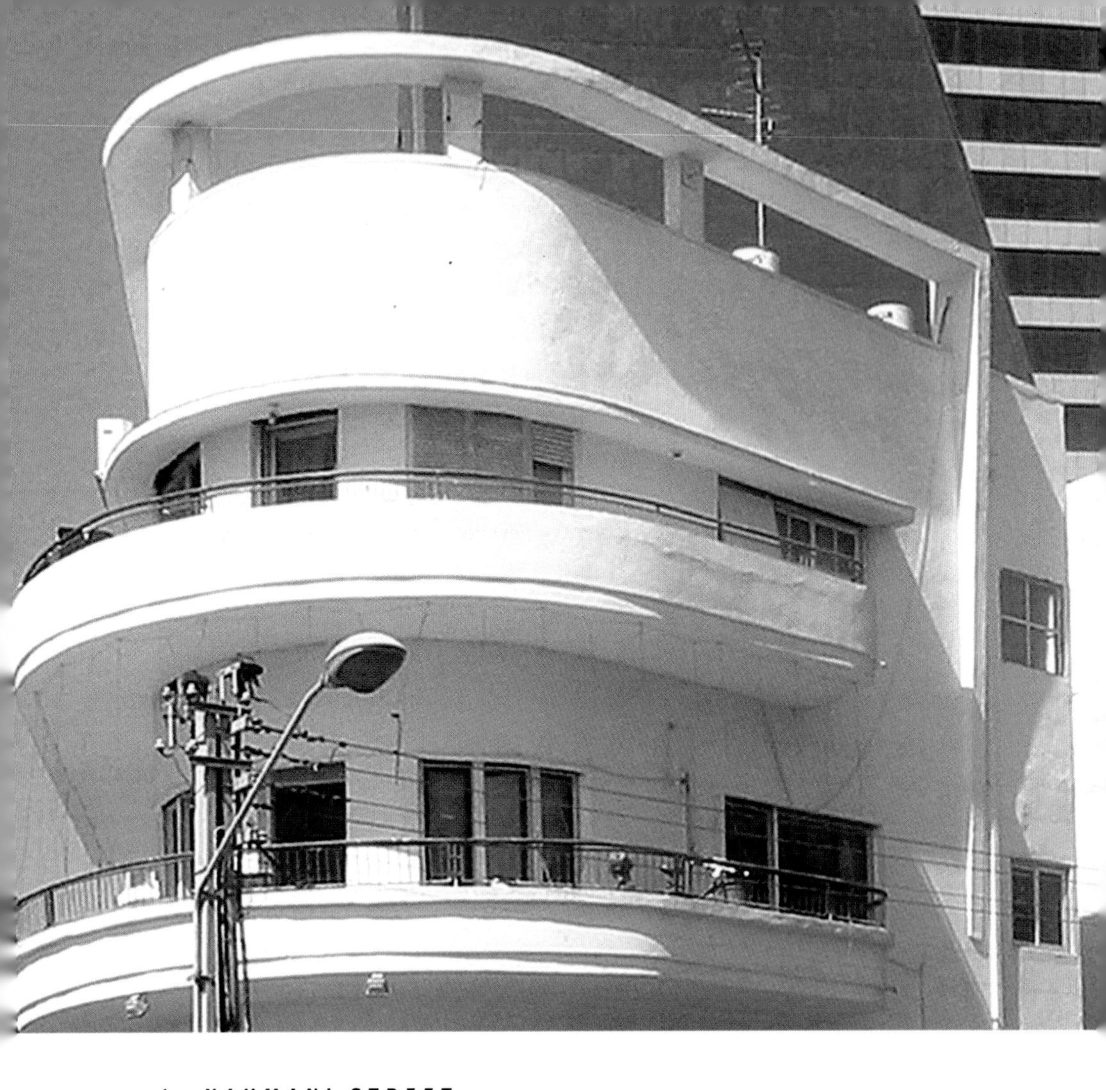

64 NAHMANI STREET

JOSEPH CASHDAN AND ELISHA SHIMSHONI BEFORE 1940

A DISTINCTIVE BUILDING ON A CORNER SITE. ITS APPEARANCE IS MONUMENTAL, WHILE IT TURNS THE CORNER WITH A MARINE FEELING, ITS FORM RESEMBLING THE KEEL OF A YACHT. VIEWED AS AN UPPER BEAM, WITH THE SHADOWS FALLING ON THE CURVED WALLS, THE PERGOLA ALSO CATCHES REFLECTED LIGHT FROM THE SURFACE OF THE ROOF, AN INDICATION OF THE CHRONIC GLARE IN TEL AVIV.

64 NAHMANI STREET

JOSEPH CASHDAN AND ELISHA SHIMSHONI BEFORE 1940

24 BALFOUR STREET

SHMUEL PLATO 1935

A ROOF GARDEN SURVIVING THE LACK OF UPKEEP AND HARSH WEATHER. THE CANTILEVER OF THE CONSTRUCTION IS AMBITIOUS, AND THE PRESENCE OF A GOOD STRUCTURAL ENGINEER CAN BE FELT. IT IS CLEAR THAT THE EFFORT WAS WORTHWHILE, AS MUCH OF THE BUILDING'S DESIGN DISTINCTION IS DUE TO THIS ELEMENT.

GLASS

Throughout the Bauhaus period glass featured extensively, often employed more than was necessary as a sign of modernity – the excitement of using new technology, opening up dead walls and letting light into shadowy interiors. However, it soon became clear that mounting and erecting vast glass surfaces was extremely expensive. The upkeep of the steel frames and glass panes was a burden and in many cases painting and cleaning were totally impossible. And although these surfaces look highly sophisticated, the enormous amount of light they allowed inside a building is not always a benefit in a hot, sunny place. Large quantities of solar heat entering a living space are very difficult to get rid of.

The examples shown here provide clear illustrations of the extent of Japanese influence on the aesthetics of early modern architecture. The proportions and sizes of the divisions look very much like those of Japanese screens. The glass wall becomes a clear example of a new flat surface, new to the West at least, designed like a light Japanese partition. Some of the glass used was specially manufactured, embossed with new motifs; some was richly decorative. Opaque glass was used as a simple way to mitigate overwhelming glare – another feature reminiscent of the rice paper used in Japanese screens.

AN ELABORATE EXAMPLE – PERHAPS THE AMOUNT OF GLASS USED IS TOO GREAT FOR SUBTLETY. THE EFFECT ACHIEVED IS UNUSUAL BUT VERY HARD TO MAINTAIN, HENCE THE OBVIOUS DETERIORATION.

23 PINSKER STREET

PINHAS HUTT 1935

A BUILDING WITH A TWIN ENTRANCE AND STAIR. THE DETAILING USES A VERY SLENDER STEEL PROFILE, REINFORCED INTO THE CONCRETE FLOORS. THE PRESENCE OF THE GLASS IS FELT, BUT THE STRONG LIGHT DOES NOT ALLOW VIVID CONTRASTS WITH THE SOLID VOLUME, AND THE EFFECT IS WEAKENED. IT HAS WITHSTOOD THE CLIMATE WELL.

26 TRUMPELDOR STREET

Z TSHUDOVSKI c 1935

DETAIL

A CAREFUL AND SUBDUED TREATMENT OF THE STAIRWELL WHICH IS FRAMED IN SPECIALLY-MANUFACTURED BROWN TERRACOTTA TILES. THIS APPROACH WAS OFTEN USED IN TEL AVIV. THE STEEL FRAME IS NOT TOO LARGE TO CLEAN AND MAINTAIN.

65 BALFOUR STREET

A BERGER AND I MANDELBAUM AFTER 1935

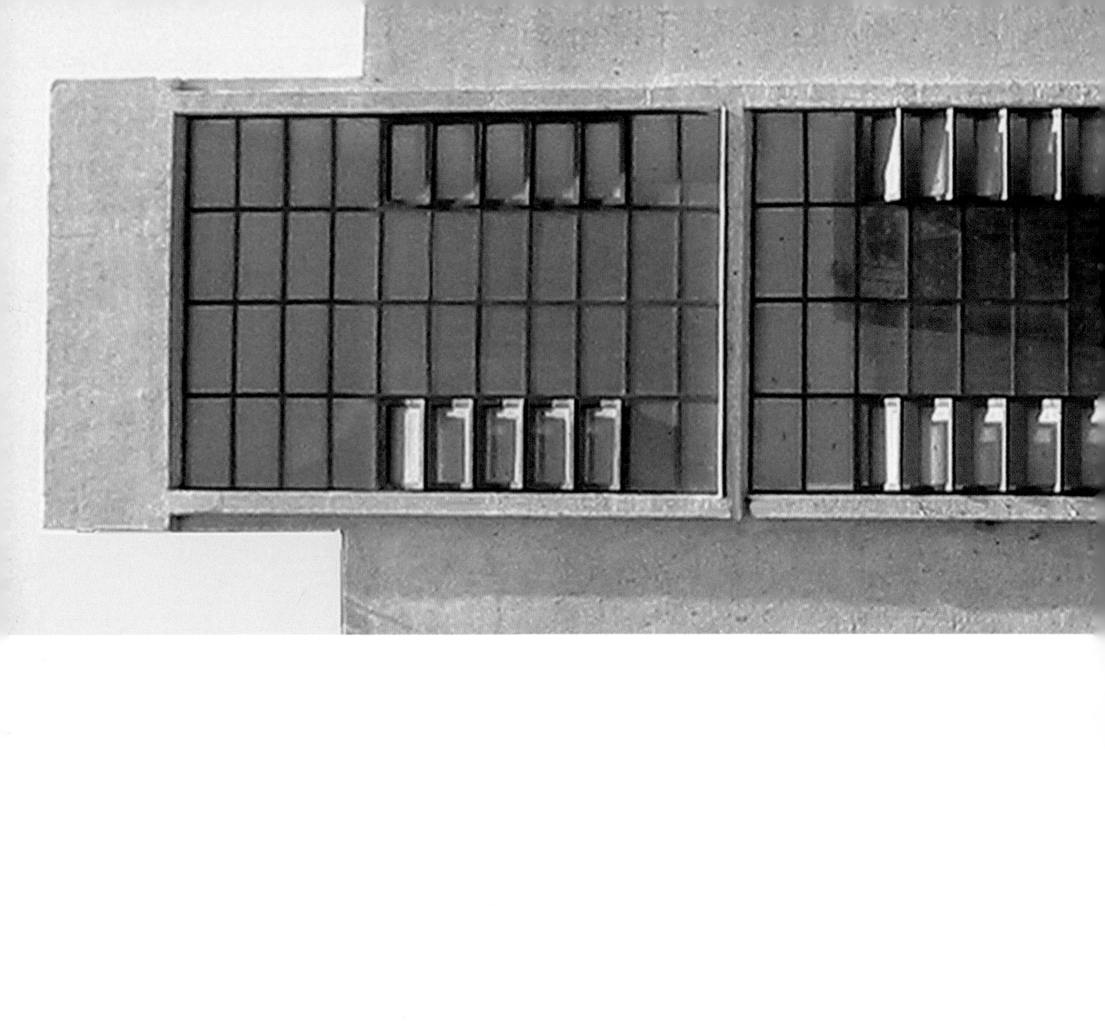

ANOTHER SUBDUED TREATMENT OF THE STAIRWELL. JAPANESE INFLUENCE IS CLEARLY FELT AND THE GLASS SURFACE IS VERY CONSIDERABLE. THE MODERNITY EVIDENT HERE IS IN GREAT CONTRAST TO THE BUILDING AND ITS URBAN SURROUNDINGS.

33 BALFOUR STREET

MORDECHAI ROSENGARTEN AFTER 1935

18 GEORGE ELIOT STREET

A BERGER AND I MANDELBAUM 1935

AN INTERIOR PICTURE OF THE OPAQUE GLASS AT 18 GEORGE ELIOT STREET. THIS PLAY OF DIVISIONS AND PROPORTIONS IS REMINISCENT OF JAPANESE SCREENS.

6 HEN BOULEVARD

J SHLAIN AFTER 1935

THE WELL-MAINTAINED GLASS IS ADEQUATELY SHADED, CUTTING OUT EXCESSIVE LIGHT AND HEAT, AND IT ISN'T OVER-PROMINENT.

VERTICAL STAIRWELLS

One of the basic elements demanding treatment in International Style buildings is the vertical side elevation of the stairwell. With its balconies, strip windows and similar motifs, the style was soon seen to be one that emphasised the horizontal. The new three-dimensional approach, whether chiefly cubist, in the round, or expressionist, was strengthened by a vertical unifying element. It is also true that the stairwell often provided the architect with a design opportunity largely unhampered by the client or programmatic necessities. Variations on the theme abound, and many are original and innovative.

The element has two functions. Firstly, it ventilates and lights the stairs, and may provide a dramatic internal effect with daylight enhancing a free vertical space. Secondly, it can itself be a light source, throwing light out on to the street or square at night. The potential for treating artificial and natural light fascinated designers.

The stairwell is also the place where lots of transparency could be introduced. Transparency – achieved through the use of glass and narrow-profile steel window frames – was a much sought-after quality. Abundant use of glass was not easy, involving a high degree of technological ability. Furthermore, the glass surfaces have to be cleaned and replaced, while the steel elements and reinforcements may distort under load and because of differences in expansion values with adjacent materials. And finally, in a sunny country glass can be a nuisance, causing glare and making shading essential.

These Bauhaus stairwells are the precursors of the modern curtain wall, innocent of the immense know-how that was subsequently applied.

251 DIZENGOF STREET

ARIEH COHEN AFTER 1935

4 סימטת מיכה
4

HERE THE ARCHITECT FOUND AN ORIGINAL WAY TO TREAT THE THE STAIRWELL. INSTEAD OF BEING THOUGHT OF AS WINDOWS, THE GLAZING IS SET BACK IN A SERIES OF DEEP SLITS. OF COURSE, THIS SORT OF SLIT OPENING IN CONCRETE IS WIDELY FOUND IN PLACES WHICH HAVE GONE THROUGH WARS, PROTECTING SETTLEMENTS AND SENTINELS.

IN THE TEL AVIV CONTEXT, THE GROUPING OF THREE SLITS IS UNUSUAL AND APPEARS VERY MODERN. THE EFFECT IS BRUTAL, LIKE THE WORK OF A MECHANICAL SAW. IT DENOTES AN EARLY EXAMPLE OF A SENSIBILITY CONCERNED WITH THE NATURE OF THE MATERIAL USED – IN THIS CASE REINFORCED CONCRETE – RATHER THAN WITH THE COMPOSITION OF THE MAIN ELEVATION OF THE BUILDING. CHOOSING THE THREE CUTS FOR EACH FLOOR RATHER THAN TREATING THE WHOLE CORNER STRIP IS AN ORIGINAL AND ELOQUENT MOVE. THE SIMPLICITY OF THIS NEAT AND PRECISE DETAIL MAKES THE WHOLE BUILDING LOOK VERY NEW.

ONE OF THE MOST ORIGINAL EXAMPLES OF THE VERTICALLY ACCENTUATED STAIRWELL. IT IS CAREFULLY MADE WITH REPEATED CONCRETE FINS, PROTECTING AND EXTENDING THE STEEL-FRAMED WINDOW BEHIND. IT IS CUT AWAY DIAGONALLY FROM THE MAIN VOLUME OF THE BLOCK AND HAS A DYNAMIC PRESENCE ON THE STREET. FROM THE INSIDE, THE FINS PLAY AN EFFECTIVE ROLE IN MITIGATING THE STRONG SUNLIGHT, PRODUCING PLAYFUL SHADOWS.

ONE MARVELS AT THE QUALITY OF THE DETAILING, NOW MORE THAN 70 YEARS OLD. IT HAS BEEN WELL-MAINTAINED, AND HAS WITHSTOOD THE HARD LOCAL CONDITIONS OF HUMIDITY AND SUN, FUMES AND A SALT-LADEN ATMOSPHERE.

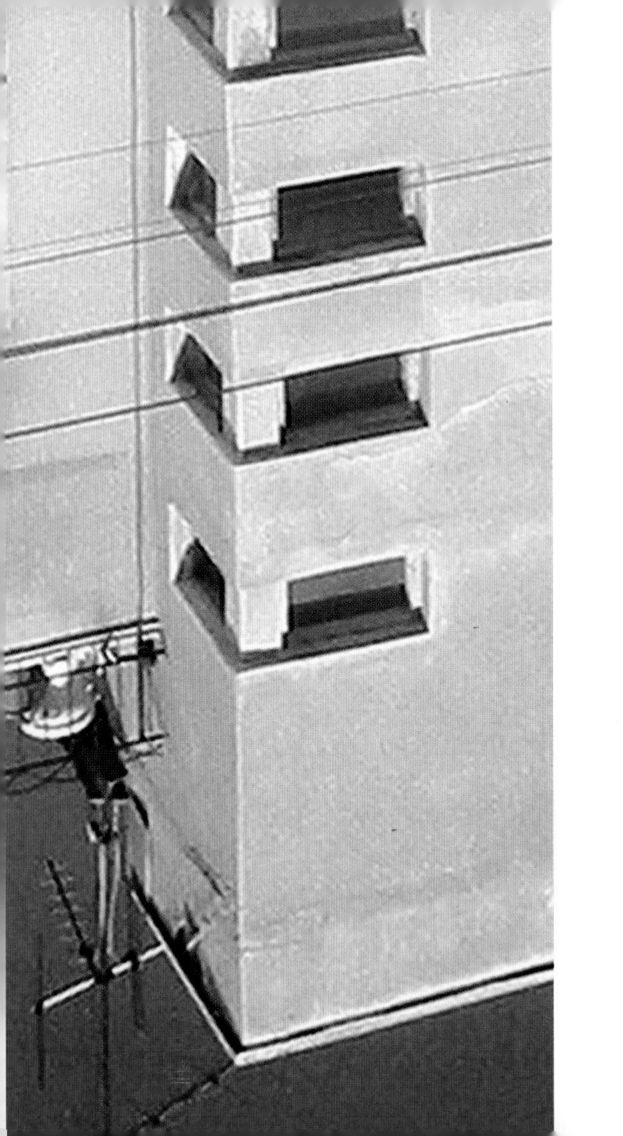

A SCULPTURAL STAIRWELL WITH THE ELABORATION OF A MACHINED ELEMENT, WORKED AS IF IT WERE A PIECE OF INDUSTRIAL DESIGN AND NOT THE HANDIWORK OF THE PLASTERER, WHICH IS WHAT IT ACTUALLY IS. IT NEATLY ACCEPTS CONVENTIONALLY GLAZED STEEL PROFILES.

83 YEHUDA HALEVI STREET

MORDECHAI ROSENGARTEN c 1936

A MINOR BUT SUCCESSFUL ADDITION TO THE VOCABULARY OF VERTICAL ELEMENTS. THE GLASS IS PROTECTED AND AUSTERELY HANDLED. SOME THOUGHT HAS BEEN DEVOTED TO ITS CARE AND MAINTENANCE. THE WINDOWS ARE DYNAMIC – THEY ARE OPENABLE.

8 ENGEL STREET

SCHWARZ & HIRSH 1936

THE FENESTRATION IS CARRIED UP AND SWUNG AROUND TO TIE IN THE VOLUME OF THE STAIRWELL. THIS MOVE IS CLEAR AND EFFECTIVE, AND, UNUSUALLY, ISN'T ELABORATED ON.

15 GEORGE ELIOT STREET

GENDLER & PIASTRO BEFORE 1940

THE EFFORT INVOLVED IN MAKING THE WINDOW CHANGE DIRECTION THREE TIMES IS EVIDENT, BUT DOING THE APPARENTLY IMPOSSIBLE WAS AN IMPORTANT PART OF THE MODERNIST APPROACH.

THE SIMPLICITY OF THE STATEMENT HERE IS ALMOST BRUTAL, BUT IT IS TYPICAL, REMINISCENT OF A PIECE OF INDUSTRIAL DESIGN. TO SOME EYES IT APPEARS LIKE A CHILD'S EDUCATIONAL WOODEN TOY, A TOY IN WHICH YOU HAVE TO INSERT DIFFERENT APPENDAGES INTO SLOTS .

THIS IS THE NAIVE SIDE OF A NEW AND OPTIMISTIC AGE. THE BUILDING IS AN INEPT ATTEMPT AT A SCULPTURAL ARCHITECTURE. ITS WEAKNESS LIES IN THE WAY THE SIMPLE CUBE IS USED TO SUSPEND BALCONIES AND BRISE SOLEILS. THE VERTICAL LINE BREAKING INTO THE COMPOSITION IS OFTEN USED. THE FACT THAT ONE BALCONY IS PROTECTED BY A CANTILEVERED ROOF WHILE THE OTHER IS NOT SHOWS INDECISION IN THE FORMULA ADOPTED FOR THE DESIGN.

3 MEGIDO STREET

JOSHUA STEINBOK c 1935

DETAIL

THE ACHIEVEMENT HERE LIES IN THE UNUSUAL TREATMENT OF A DIFFICULT ANGLE USING THE ENTRANCE CANOPY AND THE STAIRWELL. THE RESULT TENDS TOWARDS THE EXPRESSIONISTIC.

48 ROTHSCHILD BOULEVARD

PINHAS HUTT 1933

49 AHAD HA'AM STREET

ZAKI CHELOUCHE 1933

A STAIRWELL THAT STANDS ON ITS OWN WITHOUT ANY CONNECTION TO THE REST OF THE COMPOSITION, WHICH ACHIEVES ITS EFFECTS BY THE COMBINATION OF STYLISTIC ELEMENTS AND SHAPES, PERHAPS NOT ENTIRELY CONVINCINGLY.

STAIRS

Stair balustrades often reveal artistic characteristics of their period. In the case of Bauhaus-style buildings, the association with the horizontal stave of musical notation is always present.

A few technical details are worth noting. The first difficulty in design concerns the stability of the stairs and the handrail. Strength is not easily achieved, as in most cases two materials have to be tied in together, typically steel sections in a base of concrete or mosaic. The steel will withstand a lot of bending and tearing in use, but these forces have to be resisted where the the metal is embedded in the concrete. One of the best-known details here is the use of a preformed hole to take the steel, into which molten lead is poured. This is a very old treatment, dating back to stone and iron technologies. The fastening of the wooden rail is the next problem facing the designer and many different ways of handling it can be seen in Bauhaus buildings, some more elaborate than others. Some rails go into manifold contortions, looking for a way to guide your hand comfortably along the balustrade.

Other modern motifs are embodied in the steel sections, uprights or parallel bars. The role played by fashion is clear in these designs, some of which were certainly expensive and more complex than the building they were to serve. Some are simplified versions of art-nouveau motifs within a more rigid geometrical framework, some avoiding welded steel sections in favour of rivets.

In design terms, the stairs also play an important role in their connection to the entrance hall. Prominence is essential but not always achieved. We find here some common features, new materials and inventive combinations of wood, stone and glass. Examples abound and show the innovation associated with the style and the period, but typically with more reserve than would be employed in the external modelling of a whole building.

10 AARONOVITZ STREET IS A GOOD REPRESENTATIVE OF AN APARTMENT BUILDING FOR WELL-OFF RESIDENTS. HERE IN THE ENTRANCE HALL, AS WELL AS AN ELABORATE BALUSTRADE, EXPENSIVE IMPORTED STONE CLADDING IS EMPLOYED, SKILFULLY DETAILED AND FRAMED IN DIFFERENT COLOURED STONES. DESPITE THE EXTENSIVE BENDING THE WOODEN BALUSTRADE HAS BEEN THROUGH, IT IS WELL PRESERVED. STEEL BALUSTRADES ARE GENERALLY MORE INVENTIVE AND EXPRESSIVE THAN THOSE MADE OF WOOD, BECAUSE OF THE TECHNICAL DIFFICULTIES OF BENDING AND SHAPING THE LATTER.

10 AARONOVITZ STREET

HAUSMAN & BARZILAI 1935

A VERY CHARACTERISTIC BENTWOOD BALUSTRADE. IT DOES NOT LOOK EASY TO PRODUCE, BUT IT HAS WITHSTOOD THE DEPREDATIONS OF TIME.

39 BALFOUR STREET

SHEVAH SHAPRINSKY AFTER 1935

MORE SPECIAL WOODEN BALUSTRADES ARE AT 4 RUTH STREET. EXTRAORDINARY CARE HAS BEEN PUT INTO THE STRONG DETAILING, WITH A RICH ENSEMBLE OF DOORS AND MARBLE WALL PANELLING.

4 RUTH STREET

DR HUPERT HOFF 1939

THE DETAILING HERE IS LESS AMBITIOUS THAN THAT AT 39 BALFOUR STREET AND IS OF A TYPE THAT IS FAMILIAR IN TEL AVIV. THE FORMULA EMPLOYED HERE USES A PREFABRICATED MODULAR HANDRAIL WHICH COULD BE EMPLOYED WIDELY, AND PERHAPS REDUCED COSTS.

5 BELINSON STREET

SHLOMO GIPSHTEIN c 1935

EXPENSIVE MATERIALS AND HIGH-QUALITY WORKMANSHIP AT 4 BELINSON STREET (THEATRE HAOEL) – AND THE SAME BALUSTRADE DETAIL USED IN A MORE MODEST CONTEX AT NO 5.

4 BELINSON STREET

BARZILAI AFTER 1935

STEEL DETAILS ARE OFTEN PLAYFUL AND VARIED. THE DETAIL AT 8 ENGEL STREET MAY LOOK CUMBERSOME BUT IT HAS A FREE-FLOATING ELEGANCE OF ITS OWN, AND THE QUALITY OF WORKMANSHIP IS OBVIOUS.

8 ENGEL STREET

SCHWARZ & HIRSH 1936

THE WORK OF A VERY INVENTIVE ARCHITECT. THE UNUSUAL STAIR DETAILING USES A FLAT AND COLOURFUL COMPOSITION, ALMOST LIKE AN ABSTRACT PAINTING, AND ACHIEVES A VERY MODERN LOOK.

5 ENGEL STREET

SAM BARKAY 1934

THE GARDEN STAIRS AND BALUSTRADE WITH HANDRAIL AT 3 YAEL STREET ARE THE PRODUCTS OF A GRAPHIC ATTITUDE. THEY RETAIN SOMETHING OF RUSSIAN CONSTRUCTIVIST FLAIR IN THEIR PRECISION AND DARING.

3 YAEL STREET

OSKAR KAUFMAN 1935

ENTRANCES

The entrance to a Bauhaus building gave its architect a chance to design freely using a mix of architectural detail, such as stairs and doors, with paving and planting, decorative and sculptural elements, sometimes in complex relationships. It had to convey an inviting atmosphere while declaring the status of the owners and inhabitants of the building.

Some of the details used were richer than those employed in the actual apartments. Most materials were imported, and workmanship had to be correspondingly special and expensive. The aim was to create an atmosphere of ease (although the times were far from easy), evocative of European standards. The attempt at opulence was luckily controlled by the severity imposed by the rigid demands of the style. We see details that are never overdone but are nevertheless selfconsciously 'classy'.

In fact this effort to keep up appearances in the turmoil of a new country was only made in isolated instances, and in enclaves that could not survive for long. Most buildings were of a poorer standard. But the selfconsciousness of a class of Europeans, mostly of German origin, has given us lasting examples of modern design, while proclaiming their own status. This is perhaps most apparent in the entrances to their buildings.

THE IMPORTED COLOURED TILES ARE THE FIRST THING TO NOTICE HERE; ALTHOUGH THEY LOOK NEW, THEY ARE ORIGINAL. THE TYPICAL ROUND COLUMNS ARE SMALL VERSIONS OF SO-CALLED PILOTIS. THEY KEEP THE MAIN BODY OF THE BUILDING AFLOAT, IMPROVING LOOKS AND VENTILATION, LIBERATING THE GROUND FOR SHADE AND GARDENING. THE SHADE BENEFITS A DECORATIVE POOL AND A WELCOMING STONE SEAT.

81 BEN GURION BOULEVARD

GOLDMAN & MITTELMAN 1937

THE ENTRANCE AT 27 SIRKIN STREET IS SIMILAR TO THAT AT 81 BEN GURION BOULEVARD AND USES THE SAME PORTHOLE MOTIF TO LIGHT THE STAIRS. THIS BECAME A LOCAL SYMBOL OF THE BAUHAUS STYLE.

27 SIRKIN STREET

SHILEMBER & RAUCH 1936

EXTENSIVE AREAS OF GLASS AT 15 HEN BOULEVARD, INCLUDING SOME MIRRORWORK, IS CONTRASTED WITH THE HEAVY BROWN WOODEN DOORS. IT SUCCESSFULLY DENOTES OPULENCE.

15 HEN BOULEVARD

A BERGER AND I MANDELBAUM AFTER 1935

THE SAME APPROACH HAS BEEN USED IN THE SIMILARLY SUCCESSFUL ENTRANCE TO 23 RUPIN STREET.

23 RUPIN STREET

VERNER VITKOVER c 1938

BALCONIES

Balconies were normally cantilevered from the main bulk of a building. They offered opportunities to soften the usually harsh geometric mass. Balustrades gave further opportunities for innovative design. Many were designed to work in opposition to the unadorned flat wall. The materials used were usually combinations of steel in many forms and shapes, and concrete with various finishes. Proportions were often striking and innovative.

5 ENGEL STREET

SAM BARKAY 1934

WELL-EXECUTED SMALL BALCONIES WITH A POWERFUL CANTILEVERED FORM AND SIMPLE BALUSTRADES.

THE STEEL BALUSTRADE, PROPERLY MAINTAINED, STILL LOOKS FRESH BECAUSE OF A SIMPLE HONESTY IN THE DETAIL. ITS DECORATIVE END IS A SKILFULLY MADE SPIRAL. THE DETAILS COMBINE WELL WITH THE PROPORTIONS OF THE BALCONY AND ARE RELATED TO THE REST OF THE BUILDING.

6 ADAM HACOHEN STREET

ARIEH LURIE 1947

A SIMILAR SIMPLICITY DERIVED FROM A SOPHISTICATED APPROACH IS FOUND AT 50 HOVEVE ZION STREET WHERE THE BALCONY HAS A STEEL BALUSTRADE. SOMETIMES A DESIGN MORE THAN 60 YEARS OLD CAN LOOK VERY CONTEMPORARY.

50 HOVEVEI ZION STREET

KAMINZKI & IDELSON c 1940

EVIDENCE OF THE EMERGENCE OF A NEW TECHNOLOGY CAN BE SEEN IN THIS PREFORMED BALUSTRADE, MADE AS A BENT CONCRETE PLATE. CONCRETE TILES WERE BEING CAST THEN, AND TERRAZZO TILES WERE ALREADY POPULAR AND WELL-KNOWN. SOME OF THESE WERE THE PRODUCT OF A COMPLEX MANUFACTURING PROCESS USING VARIOUS CEMENT MIXTURES AND PIGMENTS .

WHAT WE HAVE HERE IS A VERY MODEST AND INEXPENSIVE ELEMENT, STILL SERVING WELL WITHOUT CRACKS OR DEFORMATION. IT IS PROBABLY REINFORCED WITH STEEL WIRE, BUT THE PROCESS OF ITS MANUFACTURE CAN ONLY BE GUESSED. DETAILS OF THIS SORT WOULD NOW BE REINFORCED WITH GLASS OR PLASTIC FIBRE.

2 HISSIN STREET

ZVI SPOKOINI 1934

AN AUTHENTIC WAY OF DEALING WITH SMALL DECORATIVE BALCONIES. THE SIMPLE CONCRETE CANTILEVERS ARE WELL-DETAILED AND CAREFULLY EXECUTED TO WITHSTAND WEAR AND EXPOSURE TO WEATHER. THE BALUSTRADES ARE MODEST.

THIS IS THE TRUE BAUHAUS SPIRIT, WHERE ECONOMY AND SIMPLICITY ARE COMBINED WITH GOOD HANDLING, SOUND PROPORTIONS AND A CONSISTENT AESTHETIC.

27 SIRKIN STREET

SHILEMBER & RAUCH 1936

BALCONIES

THE UPPER BALCONIES ON THE WEST ELEVATION EMPLOY VERY UNUSUAL FORMS. THE SHAPE, HALF AN OVAL IN PLAN, OFFERS RELIEF AND LIGHTNESS TO THE HEAVY FORMALIST BALUSTRADES. THIS ROTUND SHAPE CONTRASTS TO THE POINT OF DISCOUNTENANCING THE REST OF THE BUILDING AND ITS ORIGINALITY MARKS A DEPARTURE FROM THE BAUHAUS CANON.

A SPECIAL TYPE OF WINDOW DETAIL IS WORTH NOTING HERE. IT HAS ITS SOURCES IN EUROPE AND IS OBVIOUSLY FACTORY-PRODUCED. THIS IS AN INNOVATIVE STEEL PROFILE FOR THE 1930S WHEN EXTRUSION AND THE HOT ROLLING OF SMALL SECTIONS WERE NEW TECHNIQUES. THE AVAILABILITY OF THIS SORT OF PROFILE PROVIDED AN INCENTIVE FOR DESIGNERS TO LOOK FORWARD TO NEW MACHINE-AGE PRODUCTION. THE PROFILES ARE LIGHT AND EFFICIENT, EASILY FORMED AND WELDED OR RIVETTED TO OTHER STEEL SECTIONS. IN THIS CASE, THE WHOLE HAS BEEN MODELLED INTO AN OVAL FORM, A SORT OF MECHANICAL TURRET WINDOW, WHICH LOOKS AS IF IT SHOULD BE ABLE TO SWIVEL (IT CAN'T). THIS IS ANOTHER REMINDER OF MARINE ARCHITECTURE AND MODERN SHIPBUILDING. THE WINDOW HAS SURVIVED A LONG TERM OF SERVICE, FULFILLING THE PROMISES INDUSTRIAL DESIGN WAS THEN OFFERING THE BUILDING INDUSTRY.

3 YAEL STREET

OSKAR KAUFMAN 1935

JAFFA

Building details in Jaffa in the twentieth century could not take advantage of modern methods of production, the obvious reason being the distance from manufacturing centres in Europe. The new style did permeate through to the local Arab architects, some of whom studied abroad. However, not a lot is known about them as group.

8 Resh Galuta Street (see also page 142) is stylistically modern for Jaffa, and it has the look of the Bauhaus – with some local variations in detail. There is also an odd but logical admixture of art-deco motifs. This is well illustrated in the detailing, which is essentially decorative. It has to be remembered that oriental architecture is more decorative by nature than that of the west, and this shows in modern details.

Proportions are well managed and have a refreshing look, especially in the odd oval cut out of the projecting wall. The shapes surrounding it, such as the entrance and balustrades, are rounded to be receptive to the projecting wall.

8 RESH GALUTA STREET

AHMED DAMIATY 1936

PLANS

PLANS

The plan of a typical Bauhaus dwelling in Tel Aviv reveals something surprising: the average apartment is small at around just 50 square metres, and has only two rooms – a bedroom and a living room that doubles as an additional bedroom. Judged by today's standards, these flats are inadequate, and they are difficult to renovate, which is why so many are now now neglected or misused. Surviving indicators of the hard times in which they were built, they are hard to change or improve.

NOTE Unless otherwise indicated, plans are reproduced at a scale of approximately 1:200 and with north to the top.

PLANS

THE DIFFERENT SIZES OF THE FLATS ARE CLEAR IN PLAN; EACH FLOOR HAS TWO SINGLE-BEDROOM APARTMENTS AND JUST ONE WITH TWO BEDROOMS. EXTERNALLY THE BUILDING IS GENEROUSLY MADE, HIDING THE ECONOMICAL SIZE OF THE FLATS. DOUBLE-SIDED VENTILATION IS PROVIDED WHEREVER POSSIBLE.

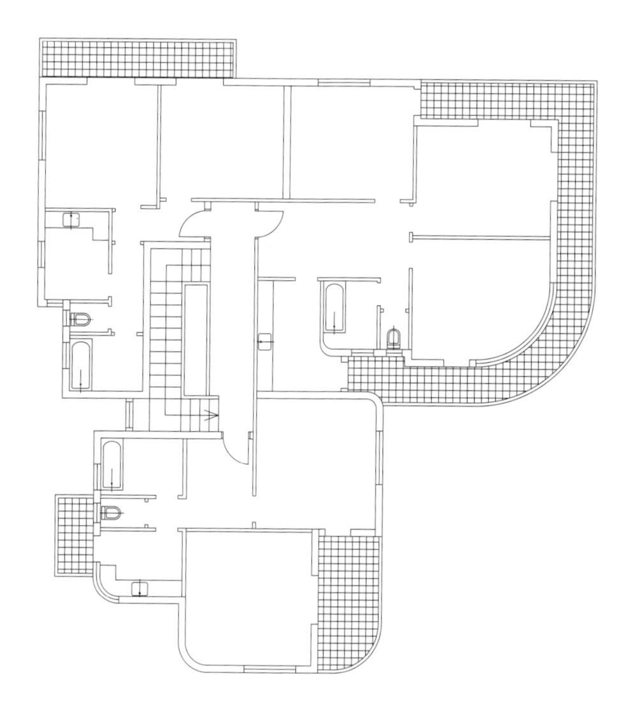

10 AARONOVITZ STREET

HAUSMAN & BARZILAI 1937

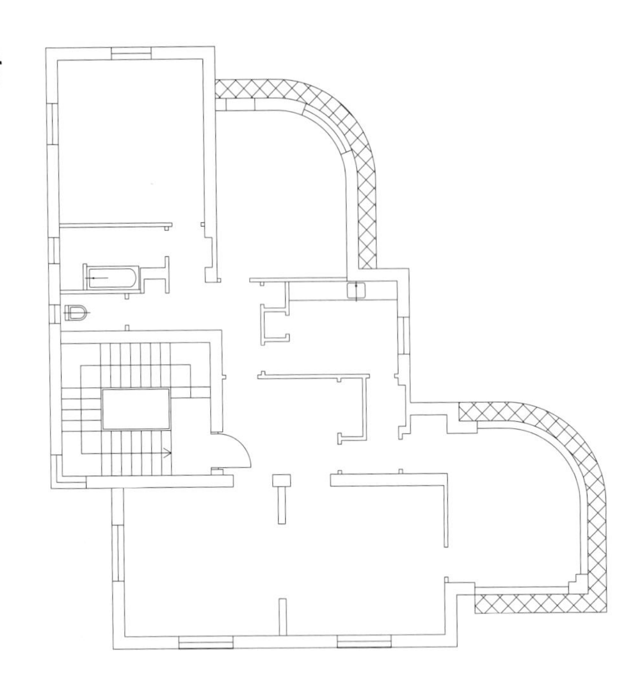

TWO FLATS HAVE BEEN COMBINED TO MAKE ONE SPACIOUS DWELLING IN THE COURSE OF SUCCESSFUL MODERNISATION. THE DOUBLE ROOM TO THE SOUTH PROVIDES VERSATILE SPACE AND ACCESS TO A SMALL BALCONY.

49 AHAD HA'AM STREET

ZAKI CHELOUCHE 1933

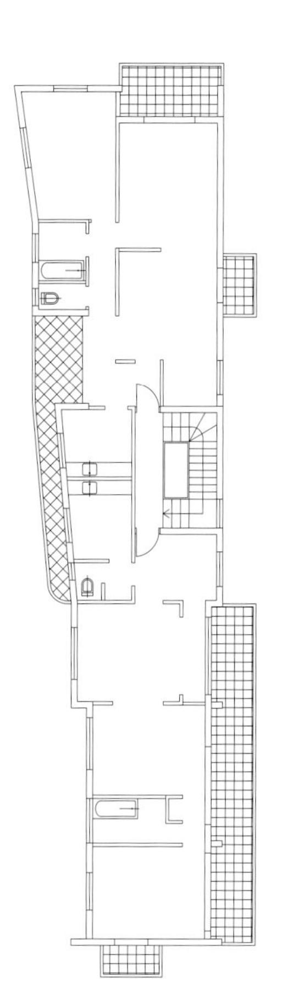

1:250

93 AHAD HA'AM STREET

ZEEV RECHTER 1937

WELL-PLANNED FLATS ON A DIFFICULT SITE. EACH APARTMENT HAS THREE ROOMS, SOME ARRANGED IN RAILROAD FASHION, BUT GIVING AN APPEARANCE OF GOOD ORGANISATION EXTERNALLY. KITCHENS ARE PROVIDED WITH A SERVICE BALCONY, A MODERN ADDITION. THE SMALL BALCONIES AT THE FRONT ARE CLEARLY ORNAMENTAL.

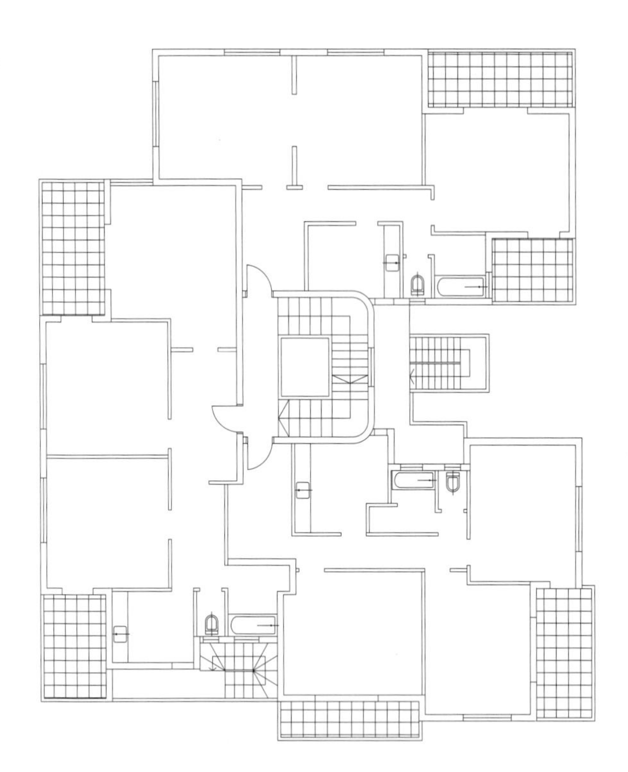

THREE SPACIOUS FLATS ON EACH FLOOR MAKE THIS AN UNUSUALLY HIGH-STANDARD BLOCK FOR ITS DAY. NOTE THAT THE THREE ROOMS ARE ALL THE SAME SIZE, ALLOWING FLEXIBILITY OF USE. THE ESCAPE STAIRS WERE A REQUIREMENT OF A SINCE-DISCONTINUED BYE-LAW. THE BALCONIES ARE LAVISH BUT NO ATTEMPT HAS BEEN MADE AT AN OPEN-PLAN APPROACH, AND THE CORRIDORS ARE DARK.

126 AHAD HA'AM STREET

DOV CARMI 1935

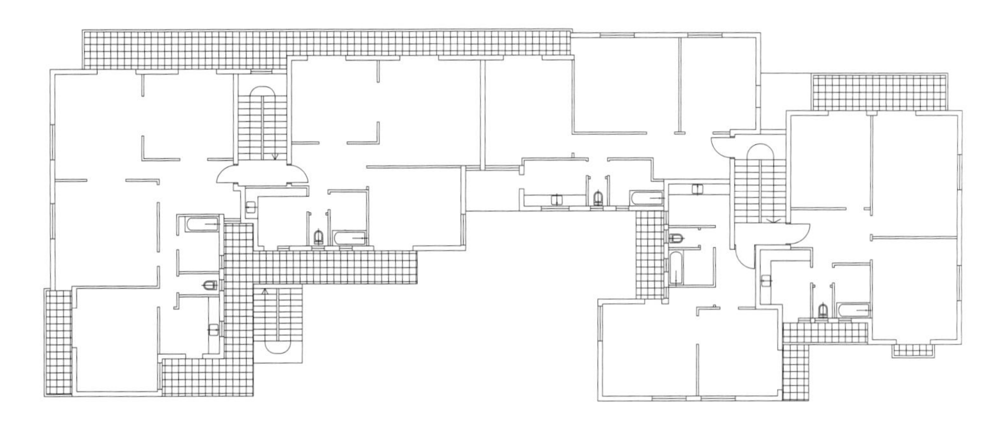

1:300

AN EXPENSIVE AND HIGH-QUALITY APARTMENT BLOCK, ITS PLAN SHOWS A MIXTURE OF FLAT SIZES, INTENDED TO EXTEND THE MARKET. SOME OF THE VENTILATION IS PROBLEMATIC AND KITCHENS ARE INTERSPERSED AMONG OTHER UTILITY ROOMS.

24 BALFOUR STREET

SHMUEL PLATO 1935

79 GORDON STREET

SAM BARKAY 1935

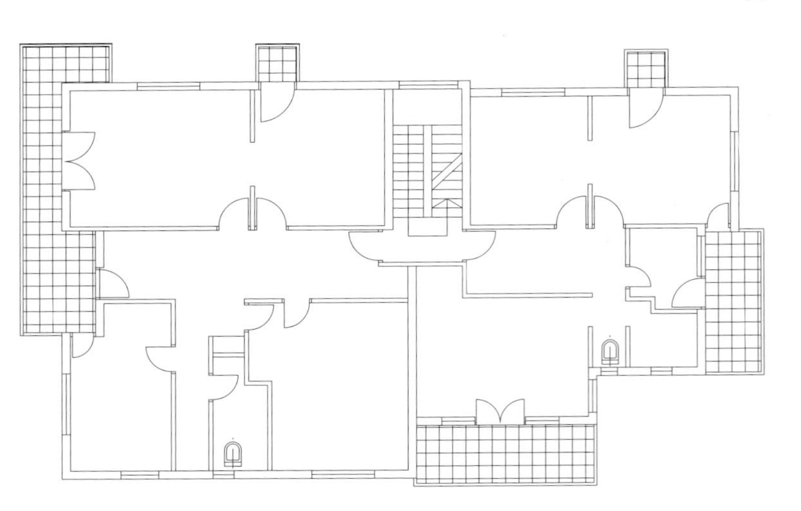

A PLAN DESIGNED FOR A MORE PROSPEROUS LIFESTYLE THAN MANY APARTMENT BLOCKS. ROOMS AND ENTRY HALLS ARE BIG; THE SMALL DECORATIVE BALCONIES PROVIDE VENTILATION TO THE BEDROOMS. THE LIVING ROOM WAS DESIGNATED AS SUCH – UNUSUAL AT THIS TIME.

25 IDELSON STREET

RICHARD KAUFMAN 1931

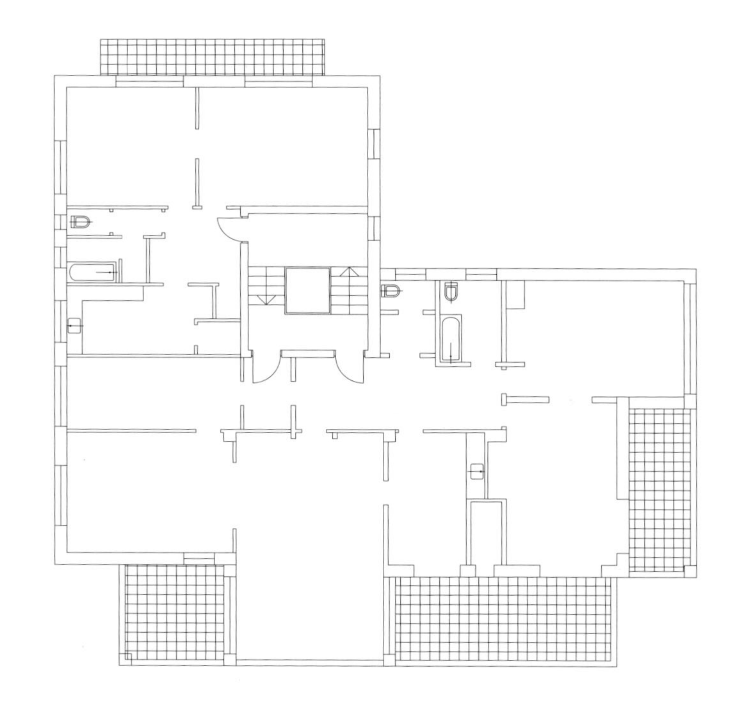

THIS INORDINATELY LARGE FLAT WAS USED AS A PRIVATE OFFICE OR DOCTOR'S CLINIC, AS WAS COMMON PRACTICE. THE EXTRA ROOMS COULD BE TRANSFORMED TO MAKE AN ADDITIONAL FLAT. OTHER VARIATIONS WERE POSSIBLE.

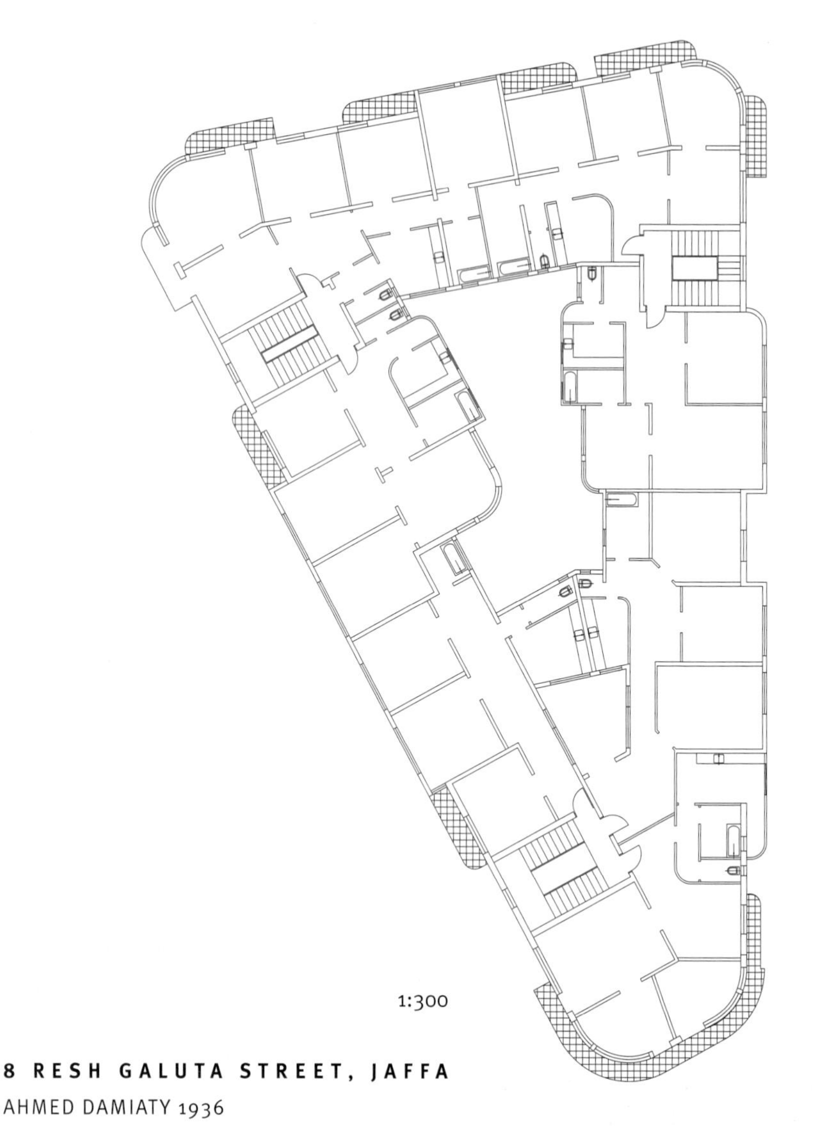

1:300

8 RESH GALUTA STREET, JAFFA

AHMED DAMIATY 1936

VENTILATION IS PROVIDED BY AN INTERNAL SHAFT OR SMALL COURTYARD, MAINLY TO BENEFIT THE SERVICE ROOMS. OTHER ROOMS SUFFER FROM POOR VENTILATION BECAUSE THE SITE IS TOO DENSELY DEVELOPED. THIS WAS PERMITTED UNDER THE JAFFA LOCAL PLAN WHICH HAD EUROPEAN ORIGINS.

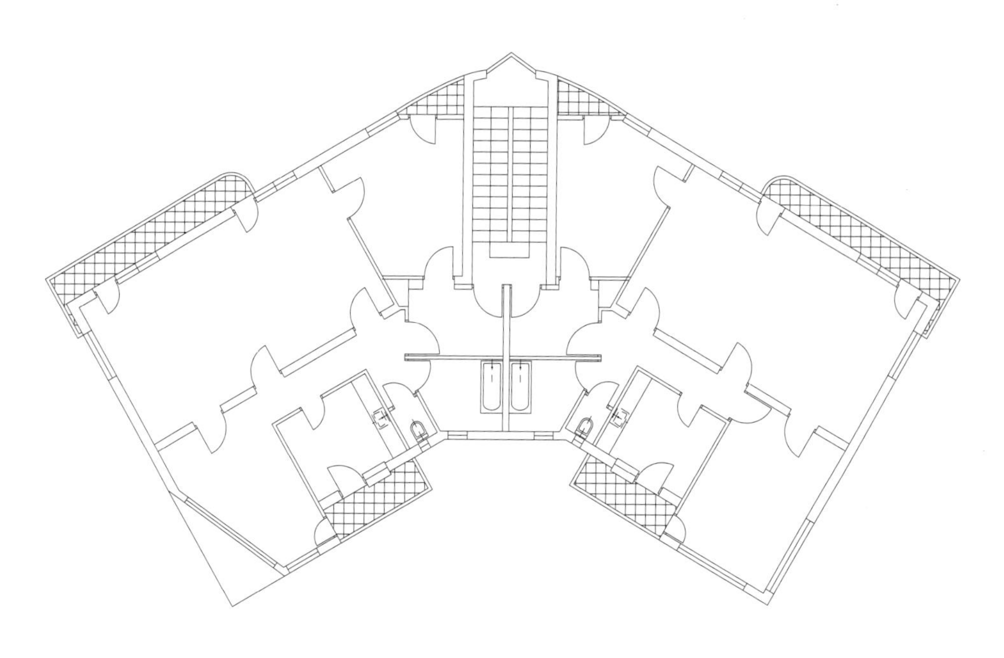

SPARE ROOMS ON EACH FLOOR WITH THEIR OWN ENTRANCES ARE STUDIES OR POTENTIAL OFFICES. THE BIG LIVING-ROOM SPACES HAVE SIX DOORS, SHOWING THE CONCERN TO ALLOW FOR FUTURE SUB-DIVISIONS OF THESE BIG FLATS.

82 ROTHSCHILD BOULEVARD

JOSEPH AND ZEEV BERLIN 1932

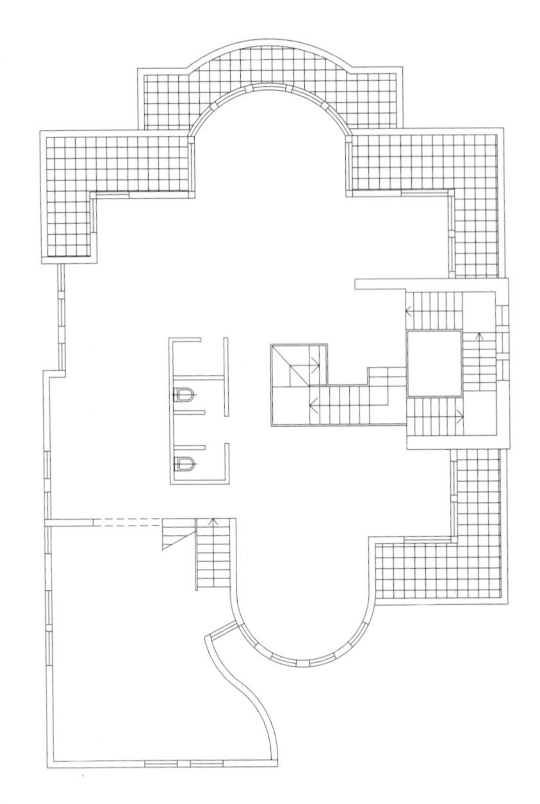

THE PLAN SHOWS THE LAYOUT OF THE BUILDING AFTER RECENT EXTENSIONS AND CHANGE OF USE. THE PROBLEMS OF SYMMETRY ARE CLEAR, AS WELL AS THE ATTEMPT TO PROVIDE INTERNAL ACCESS TO AN ADDITIONAL FLOOR. NOTE THE BACK (SOUTH) FORMATION, TRYING TO RECREATE THE STYLE.

104 ROTHSCHILD BOULEVARD

YEHUDA MEGIDOVITZ 1937/RENOVATED 1999

A CHANGE OF USE FOR A RESIDENTIAL BLOCK DOES NOT LOOK GOOD ON PLAN. THE ORIGINAL EXTERNAL APPEARANCE COULD NOT BE ALTERED WHICH FORCED THE DIVISION.

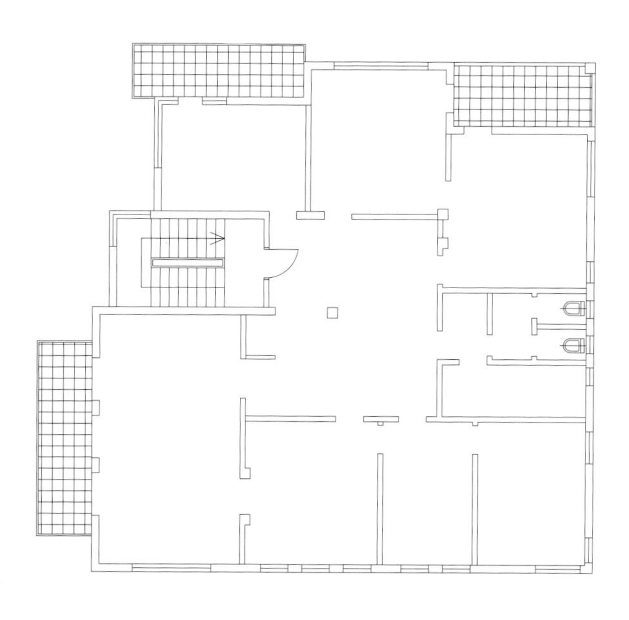

118 ROTHSCHILD BOULEVARD

YTZHAK RAPOPORT 1935/RENOVATED 1999

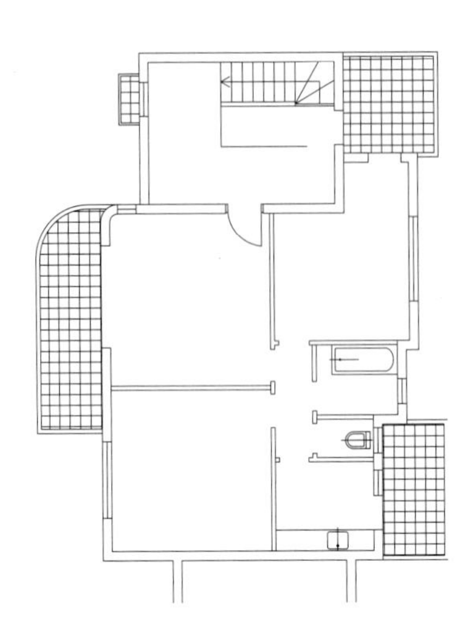

THE FACT THAT THE KITCHEN HAS TO REACHED THROUGH OTHER ROOMS IS AN INDICATION THAT THE BUILDING HAS UNDERGONE VARIOUS CHANGES, ADDITIONS AND CONVERSIONS. NOTICE THE PLAY OF THE BALCONY SIZES WHICH ACCENTUATE THE QUALITIES OF THE VOLUME.

142 ROTHSCHILD BOULEVARD

DOV CARMI 1935/RENOVATION YTZHAK IASHAR AND ALIZA TOLEDO 1999

THIS SMALL BLOCK OF TWO-ROOM APARTMENTS REPRESENTS THE AVERAGE FOR ITS PERIOD. THE ECONOMY AIMED AT IN THE DESIGN EXPLAINS THE LONG CORRIDOR AND BAD PLACEMENT OF THE KITCHENS, FAULTS THAT DO NOT SHOW EXTERNALLY. LIVING ROOMS DOUBLED AS BEDROOMS.

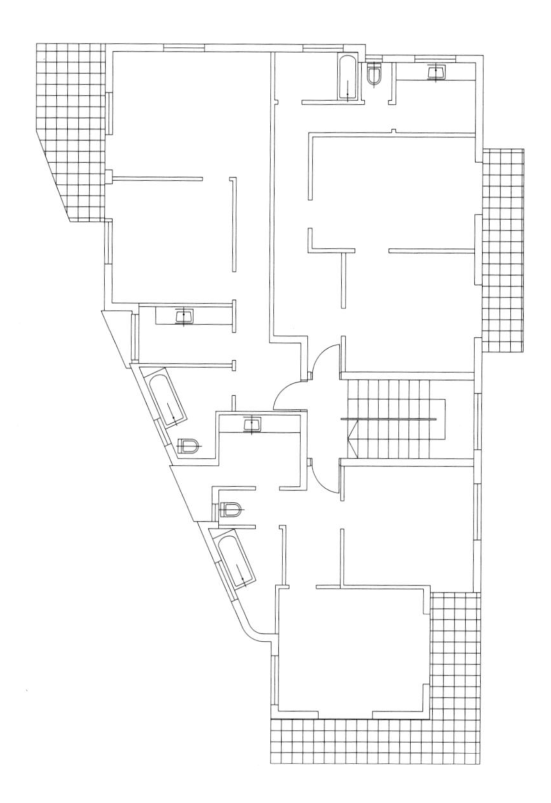

7 RUPIN STREET

MITELMAN & MILBAUER c 1933

CONTEXT

EARLY BAUHAUS TEL AVIV

The formative years of Bauhaus building in Tel Aviv are well-represented by the photograph of the seashore in 1940 (previous pages). The horizontal bands formed by balconies and verandas are particularly noticeable. Unfortunately, the proximity of the sea has not been beneficial to the poorly done stucco of the period and the present state of the buildings is lamentable. However, they are worth a look, as they show how buildings age under difficult conditions, especially when the materials used are unsuitable. It is also clear that the unusual forms of the modern buildings were not thought out as a long-term investment in durable design – the big cantilevers, the balustrades and brise-soleils are all vulnerable.

The photograph of Dizengof Square (opposite) shows its condition in the 1950s. It does not look like that any longer. Following a hastily taken and regrettable decision made in the 1970s and endorsed by a group of architects in the city engineer's department, the unusual square was demolished and turned into a series of unfortunate pedestrian bridges, a 'traffic solution' very much in vogue at the time. The predictable happened: traffic moved better but the people went elsewhere, not wanting to come to a deserted place. The whole venture was clearly a total mistake and now one might as well restore the original, as the pedestrians are no longer there to disrupt the traffic.

Dizengof Square was one of the very few public square designs of modern times, and it was completely successful. Its vestiges are the buildings left in place and now being well-restored by their private owners (see pages 124–127).

DIZENGOF SQUARE 1950s

PREVAILING TASTE

Many of Tel Aviv's earliest buildings are still standing: the city comprises a living museum, a collection of example of most of the movements in architecture over the course of the twentieth century.

Proponents of modern architecture were a minority among designers. Most newcomers wanted to see the same kind of architecture as that with which they were already familiar, or something very similar to it. Most clients and builders were not excited about new or, especially, revolutionary ideas. On the contrary, the new style seemed odd to the public, and opposition was very quickly generated.

A couple of examples – 44 Balfour Street and 55 Rothschild Boulevard (Moshe Zerner, c 1934 and 1932 respectively) will suffice to show what were then the prevalent attitudes. They are certainly typically European in flair, more specifically East European. The stylistic mix is curious, the sources of inspiration hard to guess. Locally, they are called 'eclectic'. The best one can say about their appearance is that they try to be opulent and charming and to demonstrate the social status of those responsible for their erection. This could not be more different from what the proponents of the International Style were trying to achieve: a modest, egalitarian role for their buildings. The ornamentation is typical, but its sources can only be guessed. One suspects that what is imitated here, or at best quoted, is some other imitation and nineteenth-century notions of the mixture of styles. Although often still considered to be beautiful, much of the decoration is very heavy-handed. Very clearly having only sentimental value, buildings of this type are widely respected as heritage.

Some admiration is surely due to the architects and clients who tried to rebel against the prevailing sentimentality represented here.

44 BALFOUR STREET

55 ROTHSCHILD BOULEVARD

STREETSCAPES

The group of buildings at 28 and 26 Rosh Pina Street shows the excavation work done to gain access through the newly created neighbourhoods in the south of Tel Aviv, a process that created unusual compositions in the way buildings are presented on podia. The podium – found in other parts of town for the same hasty planning reasons – is a curious structure when placed under a modern building. Normally associated with classical buildings, by accident rather than by design it is used here to create an unusual urban environment. The work also shows the original local material, a soft sandstone, sometimes very decorative and often used in older Arab villages.

105–109 Rothschild Boulevard, a row of renovated buildings, illustrates recent efforts in restoration and preservation intended to lend a new look to the boulevard, and to encourage similar enterprises among neighbouring buildings. More examples can be seen throughout this book. Attention to finishes and precision sometimes results in an appearance that seems to improve on the original.

105–109 ROTHSCHILD BOULEVARD
ARCHITECT AND DATE UNKNOWN

28 AND 26 ROSH PINA STREET

ARIEH COHEN 1935

STYLE: CURVES

Throughout Tel Aviv, a characteristic feature is the design of buildings with curved forms. This sometimes takes the form of a completely round block; in other cases it is mainly the balconies and terraces that are affected. Technically, it was no mean trick to execute rounded shapes, especially as most of them were the products of handiwork, and not pre-cast or preformed. At best, a jig was used to get the necessary precision in the plaster-work. However, the building of the walls had to be relatively well laid out, and this could prove difficult on the upper storeys. Such feats are seldom attempted nowadays, but when restoration is done, it soon becomes evident where the difficulty lies.

Whole buildings made as complex round shapes are less common. One can assume that the attraction in going for curves, apart from the necessity of getting round corners, comes from a dynamic inclination to make a building less of an artifact or the result of handiwork or craft, and go for a new sense of manufacture, part of a series of 'untouched' serially produced industrial parts.

Modernity wants to prove that humankind can be liberated from hard labour by the machine. This sometimes comes close to producing a stagey make-believe look in the resulting buildings. We also come close to marine architecture and shipbuilding which also produce large structures with a manufactured finish. Add to that the influence of the new flying machines, trains, streamlining and the dynamic connotations of the new age, and the shapes become comprehensible.

1 HESS STREET

JOSEPH BERLIN c 1933

STYLE: ORTHOGONAL PREFERENCES

A major theme in Bauhaus design is an insistence on the right angle and orthogonality, developed through many variations (and also developed extensively in typographical experiments of the period). This may have been encouraged by the discovery of cubism and by the influence of its followers in painting, sculpture and other disciplines. Another may derive from a desire to exhibit as much precision as possible, inspired by the appearance of modern industrial production. This kind of look deteriorates very quickly unless the original is both well-executed and well-protected. Unfortunately, this has not been the case with many examples of Tel Aviv's Bauhaus heritage. Scarcity and the cost of materials, the war years, the poverty of the new population, together with a local tradition unused to modern techniques, have all contributed to poor longevity.

In the examples shown here, the necessary attention has been paid to precision, embedded in the original form of the design. In many cases of restoration new and imported materials, such as specialised preservation plasters, are being used. Conservation of buildings in Italy, for example, is a progressive and growing industry that has produced several proprietary mixtures, including coloured plasters and pigments that resist the damaging effects of ultraviolet light.

The two examples at Wolfson Street, to the south of Tel Aviv, are good illustrations of the elements used in achieving the essentials of the style: rounded corners on both building and balustrade, horizontal lines, roofs finishing in a decorative beam, maritime allusions, and different systems in the ground-floor colonnade.

8 WOLFSON STREET

ARCHITECT UNKNOWN c 1936

7 WOLFSON STREET

G MESHULAM 1936

STYLE: ORTHOGONAL PREFERENCES

The prevalence of the orthogonal can be seen in the restored buildings illustrated here. All share many of the horizontal characteristics of the style, especially the strip windows and protective overhangs. Precision in the stuccowork was essential. It is legitimate to introduce a vertical accent to finish or mark the end of a composition, this being a common stylistic feature.

Another characteristic is the roof treatment in the form of a pergola or horizontal beams in cantilevered concrete, spanning space dynamically. The renovated building at 9 Gordon Street has that distinctive mark, while a new floor has been added in keeping with the existing style of the building (page 269; renovation and addition by Amnon Bar-Or).

8 HERZEL STREET

ARCHITECT AND DATE UNKNOWN

15 LILIENBLUM STREET

YEHUDA MEGIDOVITZ c 1935

9 GORDON STREET

DOV CARMI 1935/RENOVATION AND ADDITION AMNON BAR-OR 2002

A STYLISTIC EVENT

THE NOGA COFFEE BAR AT 4 PINSKER STREET

From the 1930s onwards, the cultural life of the new town of Tel Aviv was given a serious boost by the European institution of the coffee house as a meeting place for writers, actors and artists. Some of the coffee houses had an external space, open or shaded, more or less modelled by the buildings they operated from, whatever their original function, while the internal spaces had at best some newly designed Bauhaus furniture. The Noga coffee bar had both features as it was designed for its function inside and out, including the furniture. The people meeting up there were well attuned to the Bauhaus approach.

The design is both new and striking. A mezzanine floor accommodates an elevated semi-formal internal balcony, which is then extended externally to become an open terrace, allowing customers to enjoy the sea breezes. The internal double space is a unique experience in Tel Aviv, but common in similar places in Europe. Its dominant feature, however, is more unusual – an internal spiral staircase leading to the mezzanine balcony.

The atmosphere was festive and the space full of light. It could be taken to symbolise pre-war public attitudes in Europe, but it could not survive the 1970s. Eventually all the openings were blocked up to prevent glare, and the place lost its charm. It is now partly disused.

4 PINSKER STREET, CURRENTLY DISUSED

NOIFELD & YAROST 1934

INDEX

INDEX

INDEX